HR Essentials Explained

HR Essentials Explained

Prianka Jaidka

KoganPage

First published in Great Britain and the United States in 2025 by Kogan Page Limited

Kogan Page
Kogan Page Ltd, 2nd Floor, 45 Gee Street, London EC1V 3RS, United Kingdom
Kogan Page Inc, 8 W 38th Street, Suite 902, New York, NY 10018, USA
www.koganpage.com

EU Representative (GPSR)
Authorised Rep Compliance Ltd, Ground Floor, 71 Baggot Street Lower, Dublin D02 P593, Ireland
www.arccompliance.com

Kogan Page books are printed on paper from sustainable forests.

© Kogan Page, 2025

ISBNs
Hardback   978 1 3986 2433 7
Paperback   978 1 3986 2434 4
Ebook   978 1 3986 2435 1

British Library Cataloguing-in-Publication Data
A CIP record for this book is available from the British Library.

Typeset by Hong Kong FIVE Workshop, Hong Kong
Printed and bound by CPI Group (UK) Ltd, Croydon CR0 4YY

Contents

Introduction

Introducing this book

This book has been written for early-career Human Resources (HR) professionals. It gives a broad overview of the main areas of HR that you are likely to encounter when working as an HR generalist in your first role or during the early stages of your career. It looks at many of the main stages of the employee life-cycle, from recruitment and talent acquisition to learning and development and employee engagement and retention. These encompass many of the duties you are likely to be involved with in your role. We also consider the importance of developing a strategic mindset, so that as you develop your career, you can become a strategic HR partner and help to bridge the gap between HR and the organization's strategic goals.

Due to the broad nature of this book, you are unlikely to be involved in delivering all the elements we cover. However, at this early stage of your career, it's vital to have a comprehensive understanding of the different aspects of the discipline and how they relate and overlap. For example, if you are involved in an employee engagement survey, it's important to understand how this relates to aspects such as employee relations, corporate social responsibility or compensation and benefits. Together, the interconnected elements of HR drive business success.

This book may also be helpful for early career professionals specializing in an area of HR, such as talent acquisition or reward. It will help you to further understand how your work fits in with the rest of HR and how you can work collaboratively with colleagues to reach the best possible outcomes. This book may also be helpful for people managers who would like to understand more about the essential components of HR. If this sounds like you, you can use this book to help build your knowledge of people practices and support your teams.

Use this book as your companion and guide. It aims to build on what you have learnt in your HR studies, returning to many of the theories you might already be familiar with and showing how to apply them to practice. It aims to offer advice and guidance on common scenarios you might encounter while helping cement your understanding of these theories and how they can be applied in practice. This will help to build your confidence and skills. Ultimately, it will help you to gain credibility as a trusted partner who understands the critical role HR plays in helping an organization achieve its goals.

Throughout the book, you will find a range of reflection points, tips, exercises and scenarios to help you formulate your personal approach to each topic. Each tip is based on recognized good practice in each of the topic areas. The reflection points and exercises are designed to help you apply what you've learnt to your own context, so that you look at your organization with a critical eye to understand what you do well and what you could do better. Throughout, we also consider how you might be able to start influencing others in your organization to improve the approach. This will normally start with conversations with your manager, and some of the included exercises help you to consider how to go about doing this.

At the end of each chapter, review questions help to test your understanding of what you've learnt throughout, so that you can revisit any areas that you need to look at again. As this is intended to be a succinct guide to the essentials of HR practice, we cannot cover everything. The endnotes give the sources for any theory or research we discuss throughout, and you can use these to further your learning. New research and insights come to light all the time. Remember that keeping yourself up to date is critical to remaining relevant in the workplace.

If you don't currently work in HR but aspire to do so, use this book to understand more about the different elements of HR and what they look like in practice. It might help to shape your thinking about where to specialize, or whether you'd like to go into a generalist role and be involved in the many different aspects. If this is you, approach the reflection exercises from a hypothetical point of view, or consider roles you've had in the past, even if they haven't been in HR. Some of the exercises might help you in interviews, especially those entitled 'What would you do?'. These present common scenario-based questions in HR and ask you to reflect on how you would respond.

The structure of this book

The first two chapters of this book give you a general introduction to HR and its importance in organizations. Chapter 1 introduces what the function does, why it matters to organizations and how the discipline has evolved to the strategic function we know today. Chapter 2 builds on this by discussing strategic HR management and how you can develop into a strategic partner for the organization you work for.

Chapters 3 to 7 look at different areas of HR practice. First, Chapter 3 considers recruitment and talent acquisition, running through all stages of the recruitment lifecycle from job analysis and attracting candidates to onboarding new hires. Chapter 4 turns performance, compensation and benefits. We look at continuous performance management, the importance of feedback and salary structures and pay equity.

Chapter 5 delves into learning and development and how you can use this as a tool to develop the population in your organization. We look at employee training programmes, mentoring and coaching, leadership development and succession planning and career development pathways and programmes. Chapter 6 looks at employee engagement and retention and HR's role in the process. Chapter 7 is about employee relations – a topic closely linked to employee engagement and retention, and one that HR has a pivotal role in, especially when working with people managers.

Our final chapter, Chapter 8, looks at three important areas of HR work that should permeate everything we do: ethical practice, risk management and governance and sustainability. Ethics and sustainability are emerging and increasingly important topics. Ethics, in particular, should be deeply embedded in all HR practices as it's seen as essential for organizational success.

The Conclusion allows you to reflect on your current skills, behaviours and knowledge and plan for your future self-development.

CHAPTER ONE

Introduction to human resources

Introduction

This chapter introduces the different elements of HR and the important role of the function in modern organizations. We begin by clarifying some terms related to HR that you are likely to have come across before. This book will look at HR through the lens of HR Business Partnering and HR Management, as these are the most common concepts of HR in the workplace.

We therefore define the difference between HR management and Strategic HR management, and the work that each aspect of HR performs. We also consider people operations and HR as a Centre of Excellence, clarifying differences in meaning between these related concepts, and what they look like in practice.

The chapter continues by considering how HR has evolved from the early twentieth century to the modern day. It's important to have a solid grasp of this history, to learn from past successes and failures and understand how we have reached where we are today.

This book has been written to help you progress from an early career professional to a strategic HR partner or HR Manager, so we end the chapter with a more detailed look at strategic HR management in modern organizations, equipping you with knowledge of the various theories that underpin the thinking.

But first, we begin by looking at the different areas of HR, how HR can differ between organizations and the vital role that HR, in all its forms, plays in businesses.

LEARNING OBJECTIVES

By the end of this chapter, you will be able to:

- Explain the vital role HR plays in organizations.
- Understand how HR departments can look different in different organizations.
- Describe how HR has evolved from its origins in administrative management to the function we know today.

What is HR?

Human resources (HR): The function within an organization that is responsible for managing all aspects related to its employees. This includes recruitment, training, performance management, compensation, employee relations and compliance with employment law.

If you're in your first role in HR, you may find certain terminology a little confusing. The first thing you may have noticed is that many organizations call their HR function by different names, such as 'People' or 'People and Culture', 'People Operations' or even 'Human Capital Management'. Some organizations call it 'People and Human Resources'. You may have also noticed that HR Directors or Chief Human Resources Officers are sometimes called People Directors, Chief People Officers or even Directors of People and Culture.

So, what is the difference? Generally, no matter what the function or the people that work within the function are called, it and they are still responsible for the same thing – managing an organization's people and ensuring that the workforce is productive and engaged. HR plays a vital role in ensuring that the organization has a skilled, motivated and well-supported workforce by ensuring that the right people are in the right roles.

HR departments in different organizations can vary significantly in terms of size and responsibilities. Smaller businesses often have generalist HR roles, where one person or a small team handles various HR duties. Larger businesses with bigger budgets and more resources tend to have separate departments which specialize in certain areas, such as talent acquisition, learning and development, rewards and benefits, employee relations or diversity, equity and inclusion.

Some organizations have shifted towards 'People' rather than 'HR' to acknowledge that the workforce is not solely a 'resource', but is made up of individuals with diverse needs and aspirations. Emphasizing people and culture acknowledges the importance of a healthy working environment that cares about the employee experience and fosters inclusivity and belonging. This shift towards 'People' started to happen in the mid-2000s after Google renamed its HR department 'People Operations'. We consider people operations in more detail below.

In essence, however, this is all just terminology. In many organizations, functions that are named 'Human Resources' are responsible for many tasks that would fall under the remit of a people operations function in another organization. What's important is that you understand the set-up in your own organization and how your role fits in. We'll now consider some of the common differences between the different functions and departments that are broadly considered HR.

HR Management

HR management (HRM) focuses on the day-to-day activities of HR operations. Think of it as the transactional and administrative aspects of managing a workforce. For example, duties that fall under the 'HRM' umbrella would include payroll and legal compliance, ensuring that the company keeps up to date with and complies with all relevant legislation. It might also include ethics and management of the organization chart and typical employee relations activities, such as resolving conflict and addressing grievances between employees and the organization. Think of HRM as primarily a transactional, reactive function that is focused on policies.

HR functions that focus on HRM alone are sometimes criticized for being too internally focused and siloed, and not thinking strategically enough about how organizations can achieve their long-term goals. It's worth noting that in smaller organizations, HRM can certainly have a strategic element to it if it's a standalone role – this is considered 'Strategic HRM' which we consider in more detail below. In the absence of subject matter experts, HR managers in smaller organizations are expected to know about all the aspects of HR from recruitment to reward and training.

Strategic HRM

Strategic HRM, or 'people strategy', can be considered as separate function in some organizations. Strategic HRM is about creating a coherent framework for employees to be hired, managed and developed to support an organization's long-term goals. It's about looking at the bigger picture and considering the impact the external environment might have on the future needs of the organization. It involves having a deep understanding of organizational strategy including its goals, objectives and competitive landscape. In short, it focuses on aligning HR practices with the long-term strategic goals of an organization. Jay

Barney's resource-based view (RBV) of the firm, developed in 1991, provides a theoretical foundation for Strategic HRM. We return to RBV theory later in the chapter.

In many organizations, Strategic HRM overlaps with People operations, and includes such activities as:

- Talent management: Identifying, attracting and retaining top talent to build a skilled and motivated workforce.
- Employee development: Investing in training and development programmes to enhance employees' skills and capabilities.
- Performance management: Implementing performance management systems that align employees' goals with organizational objectives.
- Succession planning: Developing plans to ensure continuity in key roles and leadership positions.
- Organizational culture: Fostering a culture that supports innovation, collaboration, and continuous improvement.
- Horizon scanning: Spotting megatrends such as environmentalism and technological innovations such as automation and artificial intelligence (AI) to work out the impact on the needs of the organization and workforce.

THE ROLE OF THE HR BUSINESS PARTNER (HRBP)

HR Business Partner (HRBP): An HR professional who acts as a strategic link between the HR function and the business, bridging the gap between HR strategy and organizational goals.

The UK's Chartered Institute of Personnel and Development (CIPD) describes HR business partnering as 'how the people function effectively works alongside other parts of the organisation to deliver people solutions. Business partners work closely with leaders to help build organisational and people capabilities'.[1]

Much of this book is seen through the HR Business Partner (HRBP) lens, as this is a career path you might want to pursue. HRBPs work closely with line managers and leaders to develop and implement HR strategies that support organizational goals. HR generalists, on the other hand, possess a broad range of skills and knowledge across various HR functions, enabling them to address diverse organizational needs and demands. Being a strategic partner differs from being an HR Manager.

People operations

People operations focuses on employees' experience of an organization. Rather than dealing with transactional tasks related to the workforce, it aims to define and improve processes across the business to foster an environment in which people can perform at their best. People operations is also considered strategic, as it is concerned with identifying what the workforce needs to allow the organization to achieve its goals. It aims to see people as people, not simply resources and recognizes the importance of empowering individuals by creating a culture in which they can thrive. Data and analytics also play a big role, so that the business can gain insight into its people, take steps to address any issues and continue to improve. In comparison to HR management, think of people operations as primarily a strategic, proactive function focused on processes. Typical people operations tasks might include:

- Onboarding new hires.
- Managing offboarding for employees who are leaving the organization.
- Employee wellbeing and engagement strategies, including employee surveys.
- Designing competitive compensation and benefit packages to attract new employees.
- Developing and fostering an inclusive company culture where employees feel a sense of safety and belonging.

As you can see, much of this work is closely linked to, and overlaps with, Strategic HRM.

> **Employee experience (EX):** How an individual perceives their work and organization, including culture and relationships throughout the employee lifecycle.

> **Employee lifecycle:** The stages of an employee's journey throughout an organization, from the moment they are attracted to a job opening to when they leave, including 'Attraction and recruitment', 'Onboarding', 'Development', 'Retention' and 'Separation'.

HR Centres of Excellence (CoEs)

Larger organizations tend to have HR Centres of Excellence (CoEs) in addition to People Operations and HRM/**Strategic HRM**. These are specialized teams that focus on providing leadership and developing and improving practices and processes in certain areas of HR. For example, you might come across a CoE in talent acquisition or one in compensation and benefits. The focus is on practices and processes, rather than employee engagement and experience. The CoE model is commonly used in large organizations for support functions such as HR, finance or marketing.

> **STOP AND THINK**
>
> Do you confidently understand the structure of your own HR or people function, and how you fit into it? Can you identify which team(s) are responsible for thinking strategically, and which are more operationally focused? Spend some time mapping out your function so that you are clear about roles and responsibilities.

TOP TIP

Broaden your knowledge of HR

Look for opportunities to broaden your knowledge and experience of HR. Talk to your manager about projects you could get involved in or secondment opportunities.

The importance of HR

To understand the importance of HR, try, for a moment, to imagine your organization without it. How would you attract new employees? What would happen if an employee were bullied by their manager? How would the business ensure its people were paid fairly across teams and regions? What would happen when new legislation was passed affecting the workforce – who would know about it and check that it was being implemented? What about employee wellbeing and morale? Would that become the sole responsibility of people managers? How would the business know it had the right people with the right skills to implement its goals? And how would it know that would also be the case in one, two or five years?

These represent just a fraction of the questions that would remain unanswered without HR. Without HR, organizations would be at risk of violating employment laws. They would be unable to attract the best talent or retain them with focused development strategies. In short, it would be chaos, and the organization would be unlikely to be able to compete successfully over the long term. The work of HR directly impacts the overall success and sustainability of an organization. Here are some key reasons why HR is crucial:

- Talent acquisition and retention: HR is responsible for attracting and retaining top talent, which is essential for achieving organizational goals and maintaining a competitive edge.

- Employee development: HR facilitates continuous learning and development, ensuring that employees have the skills and knowledge needed to perform their roles effectively.
- Performance management: HR implements performance management systems that help employees set goals, receive feedback, and improve their performance, leading to higher productivity.
- Employee relations: HR fosters a positive work environment by addressing employee concerns, resolving conflicts, and promoting a culture of respect and collaboration.
- Compliance and risk management: HR ensures that the organization complies with employment laws and regulations, reducing the risk of legal issues and protecting the organization's reputation.
- Strategic alignment: HR aligns its practices with the organization's strategic goals, contributing to overall business success and long-term sustainability.

EXERCISE

What do you see as the main purpose of an HR function within an organization? Write a paragraph to articulate what HR does and why it's important. Imagine you are describing it for a non-HR professional.

STOP AND THINK

Consider the key activities outlined above. What value and impact do you deliver in your current role?

The evolution of HR

Understanding the history of HR and how it has evolved is important. It allows us to contextualize current practices and learn from past successes and failures to understand what works and why. It can also help you to challenge outdated practices in your organization and work towards a streamlined, efficient and people-centric future HR function.

The field of HR has evolved significantly over time, influenced by various theories, movements and communities. This section explores this evolution, starting from administrative theory to the Human Relations Movement.

Fayol's 14 management principles

Henri Fayol, a French mining engineer and management theorist, is known for his administrative management theory. Fayol's theory, developed in the early twentieth century, introduced 14 key principles of management in organizations. These principles consider organizations from the top down and focus on how managers can get the most from their employees. These are important to understand as many of the principles are still relevant today, especially those related to employee relations and organizational structure and efficiency. The principles are as follows:

1 Division of work – dividing up work according to specialization increases efficiency and expertise.
2 Authority and responsibility – managers are responsible for the work of their teams and have the authority to give orders.
3 Discipline – employees must adhere to organizational rules and standards, and managers can discipline them as necessary.
4 Unity of command – employees should only have one manager.
5 Unity of direction – everyone should work towards the same objectives and goals.

6 Subordination of individual interest – all employees, including managers, should set aside their personal interests and focus solely on the company's success.

7 Remuneration – employees should be compensated fairly by managers.

8 Centralization – the degree of centralization depends on the organization's size and nature. Top management should make most of the decisions.

9 Scalar chain – everyone in the organization should know who they report to.

10 Order – there should be a systematic arrangement of resources to ensure efficiency.

11 Equity – all employees should be treated fairly according to their needs and regardless of their background. Managers must protect their teams from discrimination.

12 Stability – managers are responsible for helping employees feel secure in their roles.

13 Initiative – managers should encourage employees to use their initiative.

14 Esprit de corps – managers are responsible for fostering a sense of 'team spirit' and for motivating their teams.[2]

Fayol's principles laid the foundation for modern management practices, emphasizing the importance of organizational structure and processes in achieving efficiency and effectiveness. In today's world, organizations look at the proactive efficiencies and effectiveness that different business functions drive. Despite being developed in another era, the principles still offer valuable insights for modern HR practices, especially those such as 'Equity' and 'Esprit de corps'.

STOP AND THINK

How do Fayol's 14 principles align with modern HR practice? Think particularly about 'Equity', 'Esprit de corps' and 'Unity of direction'.

Can you spot any limitations of these principles when it comes to applying them to modern-day HR? How have they been adapted or developed for modern-day HR?

The Human Relations Movement

In answering the boxed 'Stop and reflect' exercise, you might have considered that although many of Fayol's principles are still highly relevant today, they do not sufficiently emphasize modern HR challenges such as employee engagement, employee wellbeing, inclusion and belonging and the importance of purpose in motivating employees. In short, modern-day HR places far more importance on human and social factors – the kind of work that some organizations might consider the remit of People Operations.

The Human Relations Movement, led by Australian psychologist Elton Mayo, emerged in the 1930s as a response to the limitations of classical management theories such as Fayol's principles. The movement emphasized the importance of social and psychological factors (in short, employee wellbeing) in influencing productivity in the workplace.

The Hawthorne Studies were key in the development of the Human Relations Movement. These explored the impact of various factors on employee productivity. The studies revealed that social and psychological factors, such as employee attitudes, group dynamics and supervisory relationships, significantly influenced productivity. Key findings from the Hawthorne Studies include:

- The Hawthorne Effect: Employees' productivity increased when they received attention from researchers and supervisors, highlighting the importance of recognition and involvement.
- Group dynamics: Social interactions and group norms influenced employees' behaviour and performance.

- Employee wellbeing: Employees' emotional and psychological wellbeing impacted their productivity and job satisfaction.[3]

The Human Relations Movement and the Hawthorne Studies underscored the importance of understanding employees' social and emotional needs, leading to the development of HR practices that prioritize employee engagement, motivation and wellbeing that you may be familiar with today.

Maslow's Hierarchy of Needs

Another influential theory that is good to be aware of came from Abraham Maslow, an American psychologist in the 1940s. He developed the Hierarchy of Needs theory, which has influenced our understanding of human motivation. Maslow's theory posits that human needs are arranged in a hierarchy, and individuals are motivated to satisfy these needs in a specific order:

1 Physiological needs: Basic needs for survival, such as food, water, and shelter.
2 Safety needs: Security and protection from physical and emotional harm.
3 Love and Belonging needs: Social needs for relationships, affection, and belonging.
4 Esteem needs: The need for self-esteem, respect, and recognition.
5 Self-actualization needs: The desire to achieve one's full potential and personal growth.[4]

Maslow's hierarchy of needs has significant implications for HR practices. It highlights the importance of addressing employees' basic needs before expecting them to achieve higher levels of motivation and performance. Strategic HR professionals use Maslow's theory to design policies and programmes that promote employee wellbeing, job satisfaction and engagement. Other needs theorists have built on Maslow's work, and we consider some of their findings in Chapter 7 when we consider employee relations work and why conflict can arise in organizations.[5]

TOP TIP

Seek to understand employees' interests

Consider what is likely to interest and engage your employees. To do this, think about:

- Employee demographics to understand what is likely to interest and engage them.

- How you can use employee surveys or pre-existing data within the HR team to gain insight.

We look at this in more depth in Chapter 6 when we look at employee engagement and retention.

HR's strategic role in modern organizations

As an early career HR professional, it's important to understand your role and the value and impact you can have as you progress in your career. HR plays a strategic role in modern organizations, aligning its practices with the organization's goals and contributing to its overall success. Several theories provide insights into the strategic role of HR, including resource-based view, human capital theory, contingency theory and transformational/change management. It's useful to understand these to fully appreciate your role and how you might like to progress in your career.

RESOURCE-BASED VIEW

Strategic HRM is underpinned by Jay Barney's Resource-Based View, which posits that an organization's resources and capabilities are key determinants of its competitive advantage. These resources must be:

- Valuable (in that they are beneficial to the firm).

- Rare (so that having them gives you an advantage over competitors).
- Inimitable (so it's difficult for competitors to copy them).
- Non-substitutable (so that competitors couldn't easily substitute them with an alternative).

Together, these factors are known as the VRIN framework.[6] HR plays a crucial role in developing and leveraging these VRIN resources, particularly perhaps the most valuable resource of all – human capital.

HUMAN CAPITAL THEORY

> **Human capital:** The knowledge, skills and abilities possessed by individuals that can be used to generate economic value.

Gary Becker, an American economist, developed the human capital theory, which emphasizes the value of investing in employees' skills and education. According to Becker, human capital refers to the knowledge, skills and abilities possessed by individuals that can be used to generate economic value.

HR plays a critical role in managing and developing human capital within organizations. Key aspects of human capital theory include:

- Education and training: Investing in employees' education and training to enhance their skills and productivity. (Covered in Chapter 5)
- Employee development: Providing opportunities for continuous learning and career growth. (Covered in Chapter 5)
- Talent management: Identifying and nurturing high-potential employees to build a strong talent pipeline. (Covered in Chapter 3)
- Retention strategies: Implementing strategies to retain valuable employees and reduce turnover. (Covered in Chapter 6)

- Performance management: Aligning employee performance with organizational goals to maximize productivity and value creation. By focusing on human capital development, HR helps organizations achieve higher levels of productivity, innovation and competitive advantage (covered in Chapter 4).[7]

CONTINGENCY THEORY

Fred Fiedler's contingency theory of leadership posits that there is no one-size-fits-all approach to leadership and management. Instead, the effectiveness of a leadership style depends on the specific situation and context. Key elements of contingency theory include:

- Leader-Member Relations: The degree of trust, respect and confidence between the leader and team members.
- Task Structure: The clarity and structure of tasks and goals.
- Position Power: The leader's authority and ability to influence team members.

HR can apply contingency theory to develop flexible and adaptive leadership development programmes that consider different contexts and situations. Key HR practices influenced by contingency theory include:

- Leadership development: Providing training and development programmes tailored to different leadership styles and contexts (we cover this in Chapter 5).
- Succession planning: Identifying potential leaders and preparing them for various leadership roles and situations (covered in Chapter 5).
- Performance management: Aligning leadership styles with organizational goals and employee needs (covered in Chapter 4).

By recognizing the importance of situational factors, HR can develop effective leadership strategies that enhance organizational performance and adaptability.[8]

CHANGE MANAGEMENT THEORY

Kurt Lewin, a German–American psychologist, developed change management theory, which outlines a three-stage process for managing organizational change: Unfreeze, Change and Refreeze. Lewin's model emphasizes the importance of preparing for change, implementing change, and stabilizing new behaviours and processes. HR plays a vital role in facilitating transformational and change management within organizations.[9]

WHAT WOULD YOU DO?

Number 1

You have worked for an organization for several years, and have a good relationship with your management team. A new HR director is joining, and your first meeting with them is approaching. What would you do to prepare for this meeting?

CHAPTER SUMMARY

- HR functions can look different in different organizations and be called varying things. There is no single definition of what HR does, as every organization is set up slightly differently. What's important is that you know how to define HR within your own context and are familiar with different roles and departments.

- HR management (HRM) focuses on day-to-day operational activities of HR like payroll and dealing with employee differences. Strategic HRM is about aligning HR strategies with an organization's long-term goals.

- HR has evolved from Fayol's 14 management principles in the early 1900s, which focused on how managers could get the most from their employees, to the human relations movement of the 1930s, which emphasized employee wellbeing, and to Strategic HRM, which began to emerge in the early 2000s.

- HR's strategic role in contemporary organizations has its roots in several theories, including the resource-based view, human capital theory, contingency theory and change management.

REVIEW QUESTIONS

1 What is the main purpose of HR in organizations?

2 Can you explain the difference between HRM and Strategic HRM?

3 What role does an HR Business Partner have in organizations?

Endnotes

1 CIPD (nd) Business partnering, https://www.cipd.org/uk/knowledge/ factsheets/business-partnering-factsheet (archived at https://perma.cc/ S4C5-KPVM)

2 Peek, S (2025) The Management Theory of Henri Fayol, Business.com, www.business.com/articles/management-theory-of-henri-fayol (archived at https://perma.cc/DDH9-P2BD)

3 MacDonagh, J (2018) Walking through snow to get to work, *The Psychologist*, 29 November, https://www.bps.org.uk/psychologist/ walking-through-snow-get-work (archived at https://perma.cc/ ZH64-F6KQ)

4 McLeod, S (2025) Maslow's hierarchy of needs, *Simply Psychology*, 14 March, www.simplypsychology.org/maslow.html (archived at https://perma.cc/WKP8-HF7V)

5 Skelsey, H (2014) Maslow's hierarchy of needs – the sixth level, *The Psychologist*, 17 December, www.bps.org.uk/psychologist/maslows- hierarchy-needs-sixth-level (archived at https://perma.cc/ZJ7R-TXEY)

6 TheoryHub (nd) Resource-based theory (RBT), https://open.ncl.ac.uk/ theories/4/resource-based-theory/ (archived at https://perma.cc/97L2- B3YL)

7   Becker, S G (nd) Human Capital, Econlib, www.econlib.org/library/ Enc/HumanCapital.html (archived at https://perma.cc/U5S7-KBHC)
8   BusinessBalls (nd) Contingency model – Fred Fiedler, https://www. businessballs.com/leadership-styles/contingency-model-fred-fiedler/ (archived at https://perma.cc/P7QD-9DL3)
9   Malik, P (2022) Lewin's 3-stage model of change theory: Overview, Whatfix Blog, 16 January, https://whatfix.com/blog/lewins-change-model/ (archived at https://perma.cc/42BQ-8BAR)

CHAPTER TWO

Strategic HR management

Introduction

In this chapter, we consider how to be a strategic HR partner, which is sometimes known as an HR Business Partner, or HRBP. In Chapter 1, we considered how the role of HR has evolved from purely administrative-based tasks to strategic thinking that helps a business attain its goals. This chapter delves into Strategic HR Management to demonstrate why it is a critical component in driving business success.

We begin by looking at what is involved in Strategic HRM, including some key skills required to do the job well. We then look at how you can start to get involved in some more strategic projects as an early career HR professional. It's never too early to start thinking strategically, even if your current role is focused on operational work. The chapter makes some suggestions about people you could talk to, and how to position yourself as someone who understands HR's strategic role and wants to take their career in that direction. We then look at workforce planning and forecasting, as this is a key responsibility for a strategic HR partner. It involves working with the business to understand future needs and developing strategies to ensure that the right talent is in place to fulfil them. We end the chapter with a very brief look at HR metrics and analytics. There is not enough space to give more than a high-level overview. The intention is to get you thinking along the right lines, so that you can find out more and develop your practice.

LEARNING OBJECTIVES

By the end of this chapter, you will be able to:

- Demonstrate how to be a strategic HR partner, differentiating the work from operational work and listing some key skills required for the role.
- Identify some ways to start getting involved in strategic projects and develop the right mindset
- Explain what workforce planning and forecasting are, along with some key techniques.
- Identify how to start using some key HR metrics and analytics in your work.

How to be a strategic HRBP

As discussed in Chapter 1, the role of HR has evolved from solely administrative tasks to being a strategic partner that contributes to the achievement of business objectives.

Strategic HR is executed through HR Business Partners (HRBPs). These individuals bridge the gap between HR and the rest of the business. They have an in-depth understanding of organizational strategy and what the business seeks to achieve, so that they can align HR practices and initiatives with these goals.

HRBPs typically work with stakeholders across the business to develop and execute HR plans to support the business strategy. This might include a workforce plan (which we cover later in this chapter) or a particular HR initiative like an employee engagement programme (refer to Chapter 6), or a talent acquisition strategy (refer to Chapter 3).

HRBPs can also play a pivotal role at times of organizational change, when companies downsize or grow by acquiring other businesses. Times like these can be unsettling for employees, and HRBPs help to understand the issues at play and how HR can seek to support teams and stakeholders throughout the business. They might also provide coaching to those affected by change and be responsible for ensuring compliance with employment law.

HRBPs work with a lot of data and metrics, which we cover later in this chapter. They must understand the impact that their plans and initiatives are having on the business by setting Key Performance Indicators (KPIs) and measuring progress against them.

STOP AND THINK

Do you have a clear understanding of your organization's business objectives and long-term strategy? Do you understand how these align with HR strategies? If not, talk to your manager and ask how you can build your knowledge.

Strategic vs operational HR work

We touched on the difference between strategic and operational HR work in Chapter 1 when we looked at the different shapes and sizes of HR functions. Here, we'll dig a little deeper into these two different approaches to HR work by considering three aspects – the purpose, time horizon and typical activities. Note that both types of HR are essential for any business to function well. While strategic HR decisions can have a significant impact on the future success of the company, operational HR supports those decisions so that the strategy and vision can be executed. Think of it like this – strategic HR provides the vision and framework for operational HR. It allows operational HR to focus its efforts and help the strategic vision become a reality.

OPERATIONAL HR WORK

Operational HR work has a short-term outlook and focuses on day-to-day HR needs. It's a reactive function and does the necessary work to ensure HR processes run smoothly. Examples include:

- Processing payroll.
- Employee relations.
- Performance-related issues.
- Employee absence.
- Onboarding and offboarding.
- Legal compliance.

STRATEGIC HR WORK

Strategic HR work is concerned with how HR can help organizations meet their strategic goals. It therefore has a broader scope than operational HR, as it is concerned with the organization as a whole, rather than solely HR activities. It is a proactive, future-oriented function with a long-term outlook and focuses on the impact of HR initiatives and practices over the next 12 to 18 months and beyond. Examples include:

- Workforce planning and forecasting.
- Talent acquisition to fill skills gaps.
- Succession planning.
- Learning and development to help companies achieve their growth goals.
- Health and wellbeing projects.
- Equity, diversity and inclusion projects.

Skills for strategic HRBPs

Being an effective strategic HRBP involves having a diverse set of skills and competencies. Even though being an HRBP might feel like a long way off, it is never too soon to start thinking like an HRBP and developing these skills early in your career.

When you reach the Conclusion of this book, you will have the opportunity to consider your current skills in more depth and do a personal SWOT analysis to help you identify any gaps that you can aim to fill as you grow. As you read the section below, start to consider how you would rate yourself according to these skills. You may like to return to this section later, once you reach the Conclusion.

RELATIONSHIP BUILDING

Relationship management is a vital skill for strategic HR professionals. Much of an HRBP's role involves connecting with key, often senior stakeholders to understand their business areas and the challenges they face. It involves interacting with a wide range of stakeholders to gain support for HR initiatives and ensure that they succeed. A large part of building relationships involves asking the right questions and actively listening to the responses.

To discover people's challenges, think of yourself as an investigator. Curiosity and asking 'why?' are key. The questions you ask are critical to the level of understanding you will gain. Lead with open questions. These are questions that seek more involved answers than simply 'yes' or 'no'. Open questions often start with 'Why?' or 'How?'. They invite the respondent to give their opinion and provide a thoughtful answer. This is opposed to closed questions, which normally seek to ascertain quick facts and invite 'yes' or 'no' answers.

There's no point asking a question if you don't listen to the answer. Engage in active listening when building relationships with stakeholders. This goes beyond simply hearing. It means concentrating fully and checking your understanding by reflecting back what someone has said by paraphrasing or asking a question to clarify their meaning. It also means looking beyond the words to their body language or tone of voice to seek out underlying messages. This can take practice, but the best HRBPs are adept at getting to the root of issues by asking the right questions and listening completely to what they are being told. Taking this approach will not only help you uncover the issues they face, but it will also help you build rapport and trust – the bedrocks of a meaningful relationship.

TOP TIP
Don't feel embarrassed by things you don't know

As an early career professional, talking to senior stakeholders might feel daunting. No one will expect you to know everything. The key is to remain curious, ask insightful questions and listen carefully to the responses. Don't hold your questions back for fear of coming across as uninformed.

COMMUNICATION AND INFLUENCING

Communication and influencing skills are closely linked to relationship-building skills. After all, if you can't communicate well, you're going to struggle to build relationships. Strong verbal and written communication skills are important so that you can clearly and confidently convey information to key stakeholders, influence their decision-making and gain support for HR initiatives.

It is vital to keep communication going and not allow any gaps to form, which can leave stakeholders feeling uninformed. Setting up regular check-ins or quarterly meetings to report on the progress of specific initiatives can help with this. Discussing the regularity of these meetings is a good way to start working collaboratively with stakeholders and building rapport.

As we'll see later in the chapter, written communication skills are essential for developing clear and compelling business cases for HR initiatives. While verbal communication skills are necessary in all aspects of the work, they are particularly key when presenting proposals for HR initiatives to the board.

> **TOP TIP**
> Develop a 30-60-90 and beyond plan
>
> A 30-60-90 day and beyond plan provides a structured framework for tangible outcomes you would like to achieve over three months. It's a way of breaking longer-term objectives down into smaller chunks and putting some milestones in place.
>
> Consider creating one to establish goals for yourself when building relationships with stakeholders. Think about what you could deliver in 30, 60 and 90 days, starting with some quick wins over the first month to establish yourself and resolve any operational issues they may have faced in the past quickly and efficiently. You could then set yourself some more strategic goals to achieve over the following two months.

STRATEGIC THINKING AND COMMERCIAL UNDERSTANDING

As we've seen, thinking strategically is foundational to the HRBP's role. It involves having an external outlook and looking beyond the day-to-day tasks of an HR function to the broader business environment.

This involves understanding the different areas of the business, such as finance and operations. It involves keeping up-to-date with industry trends and horizon scanning to anticipate how the business might need to adapt in the future. This can help to spot megatrends such as environmentalism and technological innovations such as automation and artificial intelligence (AI). Once you know what's coming up, you can anticipate the impact such trends might have on the needs of the organization and workforce. It also involves understanding the business's competitive environment to see how the workforce needs to adapt to enable the organization to continue competing successfully in the marketplace.

An example of this kind of thinking is workforce planning and forecasting, which we consider later in the chapter. An HRBP might use data and analytics to understand workforce trends and propose talent acquisition strategies to fill likely future skills gaps so that an organization can achieve its goals. They might also create a plan, or work with talent acquisition specialists to create a plan, for how to attract top talent with those skills. For example, in a workforce where many leaders are approaching retirement age simultaneously, it would make sense to prioritize succession planning and consider which internal employees might be suitable to develop into future leaders versus the need to look externally for new talent.

TOP TIP
Start to build your credibility

You are unlikely to devise HR strategies in your current role, but it's important to understand how your role can help deliver the strategies and wider business objectives. If you are unsure, seek guidance and support from your COO or Managing Director for the area you support. This will also show that you are interested in broader business objectives and helping the organization execute strategy. Ask open questions, such as:

- What is your vision for the company or your area?
- How do you assess HR performance?
- What opportunities do you see for growth and development?
- What is the one thing, from a people perspective, that you feel stressed about, or is preventing you from getting into other work?
- What is the one thing you would like HR to support you with over the next six to 12 months?

TOP TIP
Use SWOT to develop your strategic thinking skills

It is never too soon to start developing your strategic thinking skills. Talk to your manager about how you can keep abreast of industry trends to understand your business and its competitive environment. There may be industry reports you can read, or people in the organization you can talk to.

Go further by doing a SWOT analysis. Outline the strengths, weaknesses, opportunities and threats for your industry, area or business unit. This is a useful framework for matching your organization's goals with its capabilities in the environment it operates.

Horizon scanning: The process of anticipating future and emerging trends and events to identify threats and opportunities for the business.

Succession planning: A strategic process which involves identifying internal employees who could be good future candidates for more senior roles.

DATA LITERACY

The ability to analyse and interpret data and use it to inform decision-making and influence stakeholders is a critical skill for HRBPs. It's crucial to know how to use data to inform workforce needs, improve HR practices and drive change. Insight gained from data allows you to spot trends, understand variances, get to the root cause of problems or make predictions about what is likely to happen in the future.

The tools and techniques available to HRBPs are likely to depend on the size of the organization, its data infrastructure and whether there are dedicated People Analytics professionals. In organizations with advanced data and analytics capability, techniques like predictive analytics can help to forecast future turnover and allow HR to act proactively to fill likely gaps in the workforce.

Data related to engagement, turnover, recruitment and retention is particularly useful to collect and understand. Below are some basic metrics to kickstart your understanding:

- Turnover rate: The percentage of employees who leave the organization within a given period, for example, within probation, and within two years.
- Time to hire: The average time it takes to fill a vacant position, from job posting to offer acceptance.
- Cost per hire: The total cost associated with hiring a new employee, including advertising, interviews, and onboarding.
- Employee engagement score: A measure of employee morale, motivation, and commitment to the organization. This is typically called the eNPS (employee net promoter score). It's the employee equivalent of Net Promoter Score (NPS), which is used to measure customer loyalty. Low morale and motivation can be addressed with targeted interventions, which we consider further in Chapter 6.
- Absenteeism rate: The percentage of workdays lost due to employee absences. The reasons behind this can then be investigated further to find solutions from a wellbeing perspective (we cover this further in Chapter 6).
- Training effectiveness: Measured by pre- and post-training performance metrics, this shows how training has benefited the organization (we discuss this further in Chapter 5).
- Diversity and inclusion metrics: Measures the representation of diverse groups within the workforce.

Predictive analytics: An umbrella term for various statistical techniques, including data mining and machine learning which analyse historical data to make future predictions.

Getting involved in strategic projects

As an early career professional, you are very unlikely to be devising or running strategic projects straight away, but start to consider how you can demonstrate the value and impact you bring to the organization through your work. Identify a colleague who is delivering a strategic project and offer them your support to gain insight into how they approach it. Once you have experience of delivering a project from beginning to end, you will be in a better position to lead one in the future. Eventually, as you progress in your career, you will find yourself identifying the need for HR projects or initiatives and putting business cases together for them for board approval. We'll consider this now.

Developing your first business case

A key requirement of HRBPs is to identify solutions to problems and articulate them in business terms to get buy-in from senior leadership. The first step is to put together a business case or proposal which clearly articulates the need for an initiative and how it aligns with business objectives. The most successful initiatives are those that respond to clear 'pain points' in the organizations. They address issues that concern leaders, such as skills gaps and turnover of key employees, or not having the right talent to be able to compete in the marketplace and grow the organization. Employee wellbeing is also a key concern, as happy employees are more productive. Your business case needs to clearly demonstrate why the business should spend money on the initiative you are proposing.

Impactful and compelling business cases provide all the necessary information clearly and concisely, and follow an accessible structure. Keep in mind the end audience when writing it. Avoid jargon, use clear language and keep it short, as the people reading it have limited time. Below is a quick step-by-step guide to writing your first business case.

EXAMPLE
Contents list for an HR business case

1 Cover page – give the company name and logo, date and project title.

2 Table of contents – give a structured outline of the proposal with page numbers for easy navigation.

3 Executive summary – this is a brief overview of the proposal, highlighting the problem, solution and key benefits. It should pique the reader's interest and clearly state the outcome you are hoping for. Set the scene by giving enough background and context to explain why the initiative is necessary.

4 Introduction – explain the purpose of the proposal and the benefit to the organization.

5 Proposed solutions – outline the specific HR problem you have found and possible solutions, including what would happen if no action is taken. Describe how your solutions address the identified need.

6 Key objectives – these should articulate the clear goals you are hoping to achieve, and should be aligned with organizational goals and pain points.

7 Methodology – a detailed description of how the objectives will be achieved.

8 Timeline – provide a realistic timeline for completion of the initiative.

9 Budget – outline the estimated costs, including costs for services and resources needed. State how you will keep the organization up to date on progress from time and cost perspectives.

10 Benefits – the expected outcomes and advantages of the initiative, with relevant KPIs aligned with organizational goals, to demonstrate how you will measure success.

11 Conclusion – end by summarizing the points made and giving a clear call to action guiding the reader on the next steps, which could include seeking funding, gathering feedback or inviting questions and challenges.

Presenting to the board

Once you've completed a business case, it will usually need to be presented to the board for approval. This is normally done by a senior member of the HR team, so you are unlikely to be involved in this step in the early stages of your career. Your first time presenting to the board can be a scary experience, but the more you do it, the easier it becomes.

Storytelling is a powerful tool to engage and persuade the board. There is not enough room to cover storytelling techniques in detail here, but the key elements are to:

- Start with a hook – capture the attention of your audience with a compelling statement, question or statistic.
- Follow a clear structure with a beginning, middle and end.
- Support your narrative with relevant data or real-life case studies.
- Connect with your audience on an emotional level by highlighting the human impact and showcasing your passion or interest.
- Always end with a clear and compelling call to action. This gives your executive team the information needed for them to approve the proposal.

It might feel a long way before you do this, but start to use storytelling techniques with your peers and stakeholders and notice how your confidence develops. Storytelling is a form of art, so keep practising and even record yourself presenting to fine-tune your delivery and impact.

TOP TIP
Find a storytelling course

Consider whether a short course might be useful to help you develop your storytelling abilities.

Implementing strategic initiatives

Once a proposal has been approved by the board, the next step is to put a plan into place for how the initiative will be implemented. This can involve:

- Defining goals and objectives – what do you hope the initiative will achieve?
- Identifying key players and their roles in the implementation.
- Develop a plan including timelines, key milestones, resources.
- Execute the tasks and activities outlined in the plan.

Of course, there is a lot more to it than this, but this gives you a very high-level understanding of how an implementation happens. It is always key to involve employees at all levels to foster ownership and commitment. As the lead, you will be expected to continuously monitor progress and make necessary adjustments.

TOP TIP
Take time out to reflect

Being strategic is not just about your job title. It's a mindset that you can start developing now. In busy HR roles, it can be hard to find the time to think outside of the day-to-day. Try to schedule in some monthly or quarterly time where you can reflect and horizon scan. This will help you to start thinking and presenting your work strategically, even if you do not yet have 'strategy' as part of your role.

STOP AND THINK

Reflect on your organization or team. Can you identify ways to shift your focus away from operational and reactive work towards more strategic and proactive work? Consider the following questions:

- How far into the future will your current work impact the organization?
- Is there anything you could start delivering that would have longer-term impact?
- What would you start to deliver that might continue to have impact even after you have left the organization?

Workforce planning and forecasting

According to the Office of Human Resources, workforce planning is the 'process of analysing, forecasting and planning workforce supply and demand, assessing gaps and determining target talent management interventions to ensure that an organization has the right people – with the right skills in the right places at the right time – to fulfil its mandate and strategic objectives'.[1]

Workforce planning allows organizations to align recruitment with long-term business goals by anticipating future requirements. It can be implemented in several ways, and it's important to use the right one for the industry, culture and type of business. Common workforce planning techniques include:

- Delphi technique – this is a forecasting method that relies on the input of a panel of experts. The process involves multiple rounds of questionnaires, with each round refining the responses based on the feedback from previous rounds. The goal is to reach a consensus on future workforce needs and trends. This approach allows for constant review and refining, which ultimately gets to what is needed rather than what might be nice to have. This works for companies that are looking to become leaner.
- Marvok analysis, also known as the transition matrix – a quantitative method used to predict future workforce

transitions based on historical data. This involves identifying different states, i.e. job roles, within an organization and calculating the likelihood of employees moving from one state to another (in other words, one role to another). It therefore uses transition probabilities to project future workforce movements and needs. Any organizations using this technique must really understand the current workforce and their capabilities. A robust talent and succession plan will need to be in place (refer to Chapter 3), and it's vital to have a solid understanding of the business's future needs.

- Labour market analysis – this is the most common technique as it is commercial and relevant to changing environments. It involves assessing the external labour market to understand trends, availability of skills and the competitive landscape. The first step is to collect data from various sources, such as government reports, industry publications or online job portals. Next, the data is analysed to identify trends, skills gaps and potential challenges. Finally, an action plan is created to develop strategies to address identified issues, such as talent acquisition or training and retention programmes.

STOP AND THINK

Do some research in your own organization.

- How does workforce planning happen? Is there a team or individual responsible for it? Schedule some time to ask them or your Managing Director or Area Director what techniques they use.

- How does workforce planning and forecasting feature in your own work? If it doesn't, can you find a way to introduce it? Talk to your manager if this is something you are interested in.

HR metrics and analytics

> **HR metrics:** Quantitative data used to understand trends related to an organization's people, monitor HR processes and track the effectiveness of HR programmes and initiatives.

> **HR analytics:** The process of analysing HR data to reach insight and inform decisions and improve workforce performance, helping an organization reach its strategic goals.

You will notice that you start to be asked to look at data and provide updates on HR metrics and analytics. What's the difference? According to the Talent Management Institute, 'Metrics provide a foundation for performance measurement and decision-making. HR analytics, on the other hand, takes HR management to a strategic level. It empowers organizations to make data-driven decisions about talent acquisition, workforce planning, employee engagement and retention'.[2]

Data-driven decision-making involves using data and analytics to inform HR decisions and translating the analysis into actionable insights and recommendations. Depending on the type of business you work for, there will always be data available. Some of it will be good, useful data, but some of it will need your intervention before you can use it. The process is as follows:

- Data collection involves gathering data from various sources, such as census reports, industry publications and online job portals.
- Data analysis involves identifying trends, skill gaps and potential challenges.
- Develop strategies to address identified issues, such as talent acquisition, training and retention programmes.

Below are some examples of how you might use HR metrics and analysis in your work:

- The balanced scorecard is a strategic management tool that provides a comprehensive view of organizational performance across four perspectives: financial, customer satisfaction and retention, efficiency of internal processes and employee development and organizational learning. This is a good tool to help organizations assess the progress towards their key objectives.
- Return on investment (ROI) is a financial metric that measures the profitability of an investment versus its initial cost. You are likely to be asked about this metric a lot concerning HR initiatives. It can also be helpful to think about it in terms of the contribution you make to the business. Your salary is a cost to the business and it will want to know that you are delivering them a worthwhile ROI.
- The HR scorecard can be used to align HR activities with organizational strategy and assess HR competencies and capabilities. This includes HR deliverables on key HR outcomes that support business objectives. It measures HR efficiency, such as cost per hire and time to fill positions.
- Six Sigma and Lean methodologies focus on process improvement and waste reduction. Key HR metrics include: time taken to complete a specific HR process, frequency of errors or issues in HR processes, employee productivity and output per employee.

STOP AND THINK

Reflect on your organization or the team you work in. Are HR metrics and analytics available? If they are, how can you use them? If they aren't, how can you introduce them? How might this impact decision-making for your organization?

WHAT WOULD YOU DO?
Number 2

You are looking to move into a new role, and the job description refers to complex employee relationships. You are preparing yourself for an interview that's coming up, and you start to think about the employee relations cases you have worked on.

CHAPTER SUMMARY

- Strategic HR is executed through HRBPs, sometimes called strategic HR partners, who bridge the gap between HR and the rest of the business.

- HRBPs need to hone a range of skills to be effective in their roles, including relationship building, communication, commercial understanding and data literacy.

- There are various things you can do to start getting involved in strategic projects. Identify any colleagues you might be able to support to gain experience in different elements of strategic projects, and work towards delivering one yourself from start to finish.

- Workforce planning and forecasting are key responsibilities for HRBPs. It ensures that the business will have the right people in the right roles to reach its long-term goals.

- Working with HR metrics and analytics is a key aspect of the strategic HR partner's role. The sooner you can start to do this, the better.

REVIEW QUESTIONS

1 Write your own definition of strategic HR, based on this chapter.

2 Why is it critical to align HR strategies with overall organizational goals?

3 What is workforce planning and why is it important for businesses?

Endnotes

1 Office of Human Resources (nd) Workforce planning, https://hr.nih.gov/workforce/workforce-planning#:~:text=Workforce%20Planning%20is%20the%20process,to%20fulfill%20its%20mandate%20and (archived at https://perma.cc/M84T-UCWY)

2 Talent Management Institute (nd) HR metrics and analytics: A guide to success, www.tmi.org/blogs/hr-metrics-and-analytics-a-guide-to-success#:~:text=Metrics%20provide%20a%20foundation%20for,%2C%20employee%20engagement%2C%20and%20retention (archived at https://perma.cc/P4Y5-XXGX)

CHAPTER THREE

Recruitment and talent acquisition

Introduction

Recruitment and talent acquisition are pivotal functions in the modern business landscape, as organizations seek to attract, identify, and hire the right individuals to meet current and future challenges and drive their success within their marketplace. This chapter gives you an overview of these two functions, which are often thought of as being the same thing but are subtly different.

The effectiveness of recruitment and talent acquisition directly impacts an organization's performance, productivity and ability to innovate. Ultimately, a robust recruitment and talent acquisition strategy is essential for organizational growth and sustainability.

In this chapter, we run through the main stages of the recruitment lifecycle, starting with analysing roles. We then move on to attracting and sourcing the right candidates, to screening and shortlisting, assessment and selection and finally, onboarding. As with all the chapters in this book, this is very much a whistlestop tour of best practice in the main stages involved in this important area of HR work. As you read it, consider how your own organization approaches these different areas and any improvements you could make.

LEARNING OBJECTIVES

By the end of this chapter, you will be able to:

- Explain the difference between recruitment and talent acquisition.
- Articulate why job analysis is crucial for successful recruitment and talent acquisition.
- Describe the difference between internal and external candidate sourcing and the benefits and downsides of each.
- Explain the importance of employer branding for effective talent acquisition.
- Describe ways for organizations to reduce bias in their assessment and selection processes.
- Explain why onboarding and probation are crucial stages of an employee's journey within an organization.

What are recruitment and talent acquisition?

Recruitment and talent acquisition are often thought of as being the same, but they are subtly different. Recruitment is a reactive process that focuses on filling open roles with the best candidates as quickly as possible. It involves various techniques to source, screen, assess and select candidates for job openings, often through job postings, advertising and utilizing recruitment agencies if necessary.

Talent acquisition, on the other hand, takes a more strategic, long-term approach. It's not just about filling immediate job vacancies but also building a talent pipeline for future business needs. To be able to do this well, you need a thorough understanding of the business areas you support so that you can discuss and plan their future talent needs. Talent acquisition aims to create a long-term strategy to attract, recruit and retain high-quality candidates who align with the organization's values, culture and goals. It involves creating a strong employer brand, discussed later in the chapter and a sourcing strategy which identifies the best methods and channels for creating a pipeline of candidates. It involves building and nurturing a diverse, high-quality talent pool to reduce the time it takes to hire as well as the cost.

Talent acquisition begins with effective workforce planning, which we discussed in Chapter 2. It takes this insight to put strategies into place to identify, attract, source and select the right talent the organization needs to achieve its strategic goals over the longer term. Both recruitment and talent acquisition can include internal and external hiring, meaning that the processes focus on sourcing candidates from outside the organization as well as identifying current employees who could be suitable for new roles.

This chapter discusses on both recruitment and talent acquisition processes and strategies. For example, we run through the key steps in the recruitment process and consider the importance of getting your employer brand right, which is a vital component of any good talent acquisition strategy.

> **Recruitment:** A reactive process that seeks to find the right person with the right skills for a job vacancy.

> **Talent acquisition:** A proactive, strategic process that seeks to build a talent pipeline that will fulfil business needs over the longer term.

> **Talent pool:** A group of individuals who possess the skills, competencies and experience that an organization may need to fill current or future vacancies.

The steps involved in the recruitment process

This chapter runs through the main steps involved in the recruitment process:

- Job analysis.
- Attraction and sourcing candidates.
- Assessment and selection.
- Onboarding and probation.

Together, these steps provide individuals applying for roles with what is known as the 'candidate experience' or CX. This is the overall impression someone gets of a company from the minute they are attracted to an open position, through the application and interview process, to onboarding and probation. The best companies put the candidate experience at the forefront of their hiring processes, as a positive one helps to retain talent, attract more top talent to the organization and enhance a company's reputation in the marketplace.

You may have learnt about Benjamin Schneider's Attraction-Selection-Attrition (ASA) framework in your studies. This framework explains how organizations attract, select and retain employees who fit their culture, values and mission. Organizations tend to attract potential candidates who align with the organization's values, culture and mission. They tend to select candidates who posses the skills, abilities and cultural fit needed to be successful in the role. This ultimately helps the employees thrive in their roles as well as contributing effectively to the organization's strategy. By understanding and applying the ASA framework, organizations can improve their recruitment and selection processes, leading to better cultural fit and higher employee retention. Ultimately, it results in a workforce that is best placed to support the company's growth.[1]

Candidate experience (CX): The overall impression a person gets of an organization through its recruitment processes, from attraction to onboarding and probation.

Job analysis

Job analysis: The process of breaking down a role into its specific responsibilities and requirements to determine the skills and competencies an individual needs to perform it well.

Clear job analysis is the foundation of successful recruitment and talent acquisition. Without it, organizations don't have a detailed understanding of the roles needed to execute business strategy, as well as the responsibilities of those roles and the skills and competencies required to perform them well. Job analysis collects data in a variety of ways, for example:

- Sending questionnaires to employees and their managers.
- Interviewing employees and their managers.
- Observing employees in their role.

Job analysis is closely linked to workforce planning, which we discussed in Chapter 2. As a reminder, workforce planning is the process of analysing the current skills and competencies in the workforce, predicting future needs and identifying likely future skills and competency gaps. To do this, those responsible for workforce planning need to understand the skills and competencies currently in the workforce, which is where data obtained from job analysis comes in. Job analysis provides data to inform workforce planning decisions.

Job analysis is also useful for determining training needs in an organization. If you have an in-depth understanding of a role's requirements and the level of skills, knowledge and experience required to do it, you can then develop effective training programmes so that people can perform their roles well. We delve into learning and development further in Chapter 5.

Even though job analysis is a contemporary practice, its roots go back to the early twentieth century. Frederick Taylor is considered by many to be the 'father' of management consulting. He developed the scientific management theory, which laid the foundation for job analysis by advocating the scientific study of work processes. Taylor was concerned with maximizing efficiency and productivity, and he did this through his 'time and motion studies', which broke jobs down into the tasks needed to execute them, timing and measuring each one to get a clear picture of what was involved and to identify the best way to perform each task.[2]

Taylor's work was built on in the 1940s by the US Employment Service, which used Sidney Fine's Functional Job Analysis theory (FJA) to break down tasks into three main functional components:

- Data – the information processing and mental tasks required by the job.
- People – the interpersonal interactions and communication required by the job.
- Things – the physical tasks and use of tools or equipment.

FJA involves a detailed examination of job tasks, the context in which they are performed, and the skills and abilities required. The output provides a comprehensive understanding of job requirements which might explain why FJA is still one of the most popular methods of job analysis in today's world.

Accurate job analysis is the starting point for creating effective job descriptions that attract the right talent into your organization. We'll now consider how to attract and source candidates.

Attracting and sourcing candidates

Attracting and sourcing candidates involves taking a targeted approach to finding talent for your organization. Traditional, reactive recruitment focuses on attracting and sourcing candidates to fill current vacancies. In more strategic and proactive talent acquisition, attracting and sourcing candidates also involves building a strong employer brand (discussed later in the chapter) and nurturing a talent pool of individuals whom the organization might want to employ to fulfil its strategy over the longer term.

Organizations often need to choose between internal and external candidates, especially when they have robust talent and succession programmes in place. You will learn more about this in Chapter 4 when we consider continuous performance management and in Chapter 5 when we consider succession planning as part of Learning and Development (L&D). Each approach has its advantages and disadvantages and implications for an organization's culture, efficiency and success.

> **Succession planning:** A strategic process that aims to ensure business continuity by identifying key individuals within organizations who may be able to step into roles should they become vacant. Succession programmes often involve training and developing these individuals to ensure they are ready when required.

Internal candidate sourcing

Internal sourcing involves filling job vacancies by looking internally to promote employees or transfer them from one role to another. Organizations that have robust talent management and succession programmes in place are likely to have identified high-potential employees who might be suitable for current vacancies. There are many benefits to sourcing candidates internally – here are just some:

- Leveraging the current workforce results in faster onboarding (discussed later in the chapter) and lower recruitment costs.
- Fostering a culture of promotion and advancement helps to create a healthy organizational culture and can boost employee engagement, motivation and morale.
- Promoting employees means makes for a more stable workforce. People will be less likely to look elsewhere, so knowledge is retained within the organization.

External candidate sourcing

Organizations may need to look externally to find new talent if a role requires specific skills or competencies that are in short supply within the business. Looking externally can work well when a company needs to innovate, or a team needs a refresh by bringing in new ideas and perspectives. There are also many benefits to sourcing a candidate externally. Here are a few:

- Hiring managers have access to a wider talent pool and a chance to source specialized expertise and fill skills gaps immediately, rather than waiting for someone to be developed internally.
- It can improve diversity within a workforce, which, in turn, helps to bring new ideas and ways of looking at things, especially if job descriptions are written with inclusivity in mind (refer to our discussion later in the chapter).
- It gives exposure to an organization's employer brand (discussed later in the chapter).

Deciding between internal and external sourcing often depends on various factors such as the nature of the role and the availability of talent within and outside the organization.

The approach needs to remain fair so that internal candidates have an opportunity to apply and demonstrate their capabilities in an interview setting. By striking a balance, an organization can build a dynamic and adaptable workforce that aligns with its strategic goals and drives long-term success.

STOP AND THINK

Consider the roles of talent acquisition and recruitment within your own organization. Ask yourself the following:

- Do you mostly take a reactive approach to filling vacancies, or are you more proactive?

- Do you have a policy for considering internal candidates before looking externally?

- Do you have succession and talent management programmes in place?

- Do you have specialized talent acquisition professionals who work to build a pool of available talent who may be interested in open roles?

If you are unclear about how recruitment and talent acquisition work in your own context, do some research to find out.

The importance of good job descriptions

Job description: A written document that uses data from job analysis to outline a position's responsibilities and requirements, as well as the skills, competencies, experience and qualifications a candidate would need to perform the position well.

Accurate job analysis is the foundation of clear and detailed job descriptions, and job descriptions are the starting point for attracting the right people to the right roles in your organization. A well-written job description often serves as the first impression candidates have of a company and they can have a huge impact on application decisions.

Good job descriptions not only summarize the role and outline the responsibilities, qualifications and skills needed to do it, they also sell the company by giving a brief overview of its culture, values and mission, so that candidates can assess whether or not they are a good fit before applying. Getting job descriptions right, therefore, sets an organization up for having an empowered, engaged and motivated workforce.

Effective job descriptions benefit both the employer and the employee. Employers benefit from a more streamlined hiring experience. A detailed job description will not only help to attract the most suitable candidates, it may also discourage unsuitable candidates from applying, which makes for more efficient assessment and selection.

Job descriptions benefit both employees and their managers by allowing them to understand the expectations of a role and measure performance. By understanding how their role fits in with broader organizational goals, employees will feel more engaged and motivated, and are likely to stay with the organization for longer. It can also help with objective setting and identifying training needs.

Good job descriptions should seek to sell the company to prospective candidates and incorporate at least the following elements:

- Job title.
- Job summary.
- Job purpose.
- Company description.
- Type of employment, location and work environment.
- Responsibilities.
- Required qualifications.
- Required skills.
- Compensation and benefits.
- Company culture, mission and values, including highlighting a commitment to diversity, equity and inclusion (DEI).

MAKING JOB DESCRIPTIONS INCLUSIVE

> **Diversity, equity and inclusion**: A set of practices employed by organizations that seek to ensure the workforce is made up of a range of people with diverse backgrounds, included but not limited to race, gender, ethnicity and sexual orientation, that everyone is treated fairly and given equal opportunities, and that everyone feels included and that they belong.

It's key to consider DEI throughout the hiring process. Organizations that are made up of employees with diverse voices, views and experiences are likely to be more innovative and successful. Diversity brings fresh perspectives, enhances employee engagement and retention and strengthens employer brand.

Showing you're committed to DEI begins with the job description, which can send a strong message to prospective candidates that the organization cares about fostering a diverse, equitable and inclusive workplace. Great people can be put off applying for roles if job descriptions fail to reflect their perspectives and experiences. Below are some tips for making job descriptions inclusive:

- Use clear and concise language that all potential candidates will be able to understand. Avoid jargon.
- Watch out for bias. Saying that a role would suit someone early in their career might suggest age bias against older workers. Or stipulating strong English language skills as a requirement could indicate a bias against those who don't have English as their first language.
- Avoid 'gendered' language. Avoid job titles that suggest stereotypical gender roles, for example, 'waitress' or 'salesman' and adjectives that hint at stereotypes. For example, 'masculine' adjectives might include 'aggressive' or 'ambitious' targets, or 'driven' or 'strong' leadership. 'Feminine' adjectives

might include 'collaborative', 'thoughtful', or 'empathetic' or 'inclusive' leadership.

- Ensure you state your organization's commitment to DEI in the job description.

Much of this comes down to putting yourself in other people's shoes and seeing how your job description might be perceived by those with different backgrounds and with different lived experiences. It's not an easy thing to do, but it is important to get it right.

TOP TIP
Ask others to read your job descriptions

It's always a good idea to ask someone else to proofread your job descriptions. When you do this, ask people specifically to watch out for unconscious bias and feed back on the inclusivity of your language.

STOP AND THINK
Reflect on your own organization or the team you work in. Think about how you currently undertake job analysis and create job descriptions.

- Is there anything you could do differently or better?
- How inclusive are your job descriptions?

Recruitment marketing and employer branding

Employer branding: A strategic, long-term process that aims to shape the perception of an organization as a desirable place to work.

> **Recruitment marketing:** A short-term, reactive process that aims to advertise an organization's current vacancies and attract candidates to them.

Employer branding is the cornerstone of strategic talent acquisition. It is a long-term process that aims to shape the perception of an organization as an employer within the marketplace. A strong employer brand showcases an organization's culture, values, mission and priorities. It can sell an organization as a great place to work and help you stand out from the crowd in a competitive marketplace. Getting it wrong, however, can have the opposite effect and be very damaging to a company's reputation, leading to difficulty in attracting and retaining top talent.

Job descriptions are often the first impression people get of an employer's brand. They can be used to showcase your brand's tone and visual identity as well as the organization's values and mission.

Recruitment marketing, on the other hand, is considered a more reactive, short-term process. It aims to advertise current vacancies and attract potential candidates to them. It includes activities like posting jobs on online job boards and social media platforms, and targeting advertising campaigns.

We'll now consider some different approaches to building your employer brand and attracting the right people to the right role.

THE ROLE OF SOCIAL MEDIA

Social media has become a powerful tool for recruitment marketing and employer branding. By utilizing social media effectively, organizations can enhance their employer brand, attract top talent and create a positive candidate experience.

Platforms like LinkedIn, Facebook, TikTok and Instagram offer organizations the opportunity to reach a wide audience and showcase their company culture, values and brand and reach a more diverse pool of candidates, giving prospective employees an idea of what it's like to work at the organization. Key considerations include:

- Choosing the right platform – LinkedIn is an obvious choice for recruitment marketing and employer branding, as it allows companies to reach a professional audience. However, if you want to attract a more diverse audience or a younger demographic, consider platforms such as TikTok, Snapchat, YouTube or Instagram.
- Create a content calendar – while this might apply less to recruitment marketing, developing an employer brand is a long-term strategy and requires organizations to think carefully about the type of content to create and how to schedule it to maintain people's interest and engagement over time. Content can include videos, blog posts and infographics.
- Consider how to involve current employees to give an authentic picture of what it's like to work at your company. People could share their stories of how they have been able to progress, or those from diverse backgrounds could describe initiatives that make them feel like they belong – we delve into this more in the next section.
- Recruitment marketing can leverage targeted advertising campaigns, whereby you pay for ads to reach specific demographics and job seekers with the skills and experience you are looking for.

Ideally, you want your social media engagement to translate into followers who continue to interact with your brand by participating in industry discussions and building a positive online presence.

EXERCISE

How does your organization use social media to build its employer brand? Do you have a clear strategy in place in terms of platforms and content schedules? Analyse your approach and list one to three ways that you could improve.

USING ROLE MODELS AND AMBASSADORS

Role models and ambassadors play a crucial role in promoting an organization's employer brand and showcasing its values, work environment and culture. The most effective way to do this is by asking individuals to share their experiences through storytelling.

Storytelling is a powerful tool which, when used effectively, can transform people's perceptions (or misperceptions) of organizations. Narratives need to be authentic to have the greatest effect, so the less scripted, the better. The aim is to tell stories that resonate with your target audience, so when choosing your role models and ambassadors, consider demographics and diversity carefully so that you reflect a range of experiences and backgrounds within your company that your target audience will be able to relate to. Also, aim to choose individuals who are personable, warm and able to engage people and build trust through the stories that they tell. You need people who are enthusiastic and engaged – look for those who have been with the company for a long time and take on work outside the core duties for their role, for example, those who regularly put their hand up to head up initiatives. It might sound obvious, but you will also need people who are already active on social media and have large followings, so that you can reach a large audience through the content they create.

TOP TIP
Don't overlook Glassdoor

Glassdoor is a job search and career community website where users can anonymously review their organizations, including giving salary information. Negative reviews on Glassdoor can be very damaging to an employer's brand, but the opposite is also true.

Consider using Glassdoor to showcase a positive employee experience through your brand ambassadors and role models.

EVENTS AND CAREER FAIRS

Hosting or participating in industry events such as career fairs or networking sessions also provides organizations with an opportunity to connect with potential candidates and showcase their employer brand. Below are some reasons why organizations choose to attend in-person events on top of their online activity:

- Access to a wider talent pool – we all have different preferences, and some people prefer to attend job fairs and events rather than spend time on social media. Doing both allows organizations to access the widest possible pool of potential candidates.
- Increase your brand visibility – a physical presence at events and fairs will reinforce your brand, making you more memorable and keeping you top-of-mind for potential candidates.
- Direct access with candidates – enhances your understanding of potential candidates and what they are looking for in a job and an employer. It also allows you to assess potential candidates' skills and experience, and gain feedback about perceptions of your employer brand.

> **TOP TIP**
>
> Attend recruitment or industry events
>
> Research recruitment and industry-specific events in your local area over the next few months. Identify one or two that you could attend. Aim to connect with others, learn from them and gain a better understanding of your market. Ultimately, aim to use these events to build a pipeline of new talent.

Assessment and selection

> **Assessment:** A process that evaluates a candidate's suitability for a role through various methods.

> **Selection:** The process of selecting a successful candidate based on the assessment process.

Assessment and selection are the next stages of the recruitment process after attraction and sourcing. Once candidates have been attracted to a job, they are assessed through a variety of methods and, eventually, the most suitable candidate is selected and offered the job.

Before candidates are assessed, they go through a screening process, which is the first step that filters out unsuitable candidates before assessment processes begin. Screening can be done through manual or automated methods (increasingly using AI to filter according to keywords) and involves reviewing CVs, covering letters, and, sometimes, initial interviews to do very basic skills checks before progressing to assessment.

Assessing candidates can be done through a variety of methods and tools, including those mentioned below. The best approaches use a combination of these methods to objectively and fairly assess candidates.

Reviewing CVs and covering letters

Relying on CVs and covering letters is still commonplace, but it's increasingly considered to be an outdated method, as it is so open to introducing bias, whether conscious or unconscious (more on bias below). People may unintentionally (or intentionally!) make judgements based on a candidate's name, age, location, race, gender or university, so solely using this assessment method is not generally advised. Some more forward-thinking organizations use blind (or anonymized) CVs where all personal information is removed.

Online skills tests

Online skills tests can be used to assess technical skills needed for a job, for example, coding or writing skills or numerical reasoning.

Online psychometric testing

Tests which are designed to measure candidates' cognitive abilities, knowledge, behavioural traits and personality.

Assessment centres

Assessment centres allow employers to view candidates in real-world situations that mirror those they would be in in their role. They typically involve a variety of activities such as group exercises, role play or presentations.

In-person task tests

These are role-specific tasks candidates are asked to perform to assess how they are likely to perform in the job. Examples include drafting a social media campaign or writing a proposal.

Interviews

There are many different types of interviews. They can be performed in-person or virtually via video call or phone. Candidates can be interviewed by just one person, two people or a panel of people. There can also be several rounds of interviews with different stakeholders in an organization.

The fairest form of interview is arguably a structured interview, in which every candidate is asked the same set of questions and a standardized scoring system is used to evaluate each one. This is perhaps the fairest way of making comparisons between different candidates. Unstructured interviews, on the other hand, are exactly how they sound. The interviewer does not need to stick to a standard set of questions, and can allow the conversation to lead where it leads. This method is more relaxed and may allow the interviewer to get to know each candidate better, but it does not allow for objective and clear comparison between candidates.

Ensuring fairness in assessment and selection

Organizations should strive to ensure fairness and equity in their assessment and selection processes. Many organizations rely too heavily on subjective hiring processes which are subject to conscious or unconscious bias. By implementing methods such as blind CVs, structured interviews, using objective and consistent selection criteria and psychometric testing, organizations can be sure that they are giving every candidate a fair and equal chance of getting the job.

STOP AND THINK

How fair and transparent are your hiring processes? Doing some research, if necessary, discover whether your organization uses any of the following:

- Blind CVs.
- Structured interviews.
- Online psychometric testing.

If you feel your recruitment practices are unfair, can you see the impact of this on your organization's culture?

TOP TIP
Keep up to date with technology

Research the most up-to-date technologies on the market used in assessment and selection, and compare that to what you use in your organization. Could you make any suggestions for improvement?

Onboarding and probation

Onboarding: The process of welcoming new employees into the organization, starting as soon as an offer has been made. Typical onboarding seeks to introduce an employee to their role, organizational processes and culture.

Probation: Sometimes known as a trial period, this starts at the beginning of an employee's contract and allows the employer and employee to assess the employee's compatibility with the role and company over a specified period.

Onboarding and probation are the first stages of an employee's journey. Both processes require investment from the employee and employer. Doing them thoughtfully and well demonstrates the organization's commitment to its workforce.

It's particularly important that organizations have effective and engaging onboarding processes to set employees up for a successful future in the company and allow them to acclimatize to their new role, company and colleagues. A typical onboarding process includes two stages:

- Pre-boarding – this is the period of time between someone being offered a role and their first day at the company. It's crucial for employers to stay in touch during this time, to foster a sense of belonging from the start. It's also good to use this time to set employees up with their IT details, ask them to complete necessary paperwork or share useful information such as what to expect on their first day, or parking or train station details. If your organization has a buddy scheme for welcoming employees, you could introduce the new hire to their mentor during this time.
- Orientation/induction – this begins on day 1 and is focused on introducing new hires to such things as company policies, mission and values and providing access to necessary tools, systems and resources the person will need to perform their job. It often involves role-specific training to ensure the new hire can perform their duties effectively. Creating opportunities for employees to connect with colleagues is a significant aspect of onboarding and should always be worked into orientation schedules.

TOP TIP
Establish a mentoring or buddy programme for new hires

Establishing mentorship programmes or buddy systems where experienced employees guide new starters reinforces the company's commitment to employee development and growth and enables the new hire to learn about the organization more quickly.

The probation period typically begins simultaneously with onboarding. Its length depends on the organization and ranges from a few weeks to six months, depending on the role and company policies. The probation period benefits both the employer and the employee. The employer can evaluate the suitability of a new hire for their role and the company, while the employee can see if the job and company meet their expectations and assess their own compatibility and performance within a set framework. Beyond performance, it's important to assess alignment with company values and team dynamics. It is usually easier to terminate employment during the probation period than once it has ended, with shorter notice periods.

It's crucial to set clear objectives and performance metrics during probation so that both the employer and employee can evaluate their progress and performance. Providing feedback from the start ensures the employee understands expectations and feels comfortable voicing questions or concerns. The importance of feedback is covered in more depth in Chapter 4.

STOP AND THINK

Reflect on your own organization or the team that you work in.

- Is there currently a good probation process in place? If not, could you take the lead on introducing one?
- Do all managers receive training on probation?

TOP TIP
Analyse your recruitment processes

Organizations can get stuck using tried and tested recruitment practices that have worked for years, which can sometimes mean they aren't willing to look for new methods that might improve or streamline things, or make recruitment fairer.

Do your own analysis over the next three to six months, even if recruitment isn't your specialism or part of your role. Seek to find better or more innovative ways to recruit new talent to add value to your organization.

WHAT WOULD YOU DO?
Number 3

A manager has a new starter who interviewed well but is not performing to the level expected. The manager asks you for advice on how to approach the conversation.

- What would you advise them to say?
- What other advice would you offer the manager?

CHAPTER SUMMARY

- Recruitment and talent acquisition are not the same thing. Recruitment is a short-term, reactive process which focuses on filling open positions. Talent acquisition is a longer-term more strategic process which aims to ensure the organization has a pipeline of top talent to meet its future needs.

- The steps involved in recruitment combine to form the candidate experience. Focusing on providing a good candidate experience helps an employer's brand and enables it to continue to attract top talent.

- Job analysis provides a detailed understanding of the roles required to execute an organization's strategy, as well as the skills, competencies and experience individuals need to do the roles well.

- Candidates can be sourced internally and externally, and there are benefits to both approaches. Generally, it's good to look internally first to foster engagement and motivation in the workforce.

- Building a strong employer brand is crucial for attracting the right talent to your organization.
- The assessment and selection process is often open to subjective bias. Organizations must strive to implement practices that allow for objective and fair comparison of candidates.
- Onboarding and probation are the first stages of an employee's journey. It's crucial to get them right and prioritize introducing employees to the company's culture and values as well as internal processes.

REVIEW QUESTIONS

1 Write your own definitions of recruitment and talent acquisition, based on this chapter.

2 Why is it important to balance the need for filling vacancies with building a long-term talent pipeline?

3 Explain the role of employer branding in talent acquisition.

4 List three ways that employers can reduce bias and increase fairness in their assessment and section processes.

Endnotes

1 Schneider, B, Smith, D B and Goldstein H W (2000) Attraction–Selection–Attrition: Toward a person–environment psychology of organizations. In Walsh, W B, Craik, K H and Price, R H (eds), *Person–Environment Psychology* (2nd edition), Lawrence Erlbaum Associates Publishers

2 Peek, S (2025) The management theory of Frederick Taylor, Business.com, 16 January, https://www.business.com/articles/management-theory-of-frederick-taylor (archived at https://perma.cc/AJ7B-7ANB)

CHAPTER FOUR

Performance, compensation and benefits

Introduction

In Chapter 3, we considered some of the methods organizations use to attract top talent. This chapter further considers how organizations continuously redefine how they attract, retain, and empower talent through performance management and compensation and benefits packages. As organizations navigate increasing complexity and shifting employee expectations, three key pillars take centre stage: continuous performance management with effective feedback and coaching, salary structures and pay equity, and comprehensive benefits packages. Together, these elements form the foundation of a thriving, equitable and high-performing workplace, and we consider each of them in turn in this chapter.

While managers are directly responsible for the performance of their teams, this chapter demonstrates that HR plays a key role in defining performance management processes and methods and supporting managers to give effective feedback and coaching to their teams. HR's main role in compensation and benefits is to ensure that an organization's offering is competitive and that pay and benefits are consistent and fair across the organization.

LEARNING OBJECTIVES

By the end of this chapter, you will be able to:

- Explain the benefits of continuous performance management over traditional annual reviews.
- Describe how 360-degree feedback can be a powerful tool for personal and professional growth.
- Articulate how coaching for development empowers employees.
- Describe different salary structures and why sharing them is a good idea.
- Understand the relationship between performance management, compensation and benefits.

Managing performance

Organizations expect individuals to perform to the best of their ability and contribute towards business-related goals. Performance management is critical to this aim. Contrary to what some believe, managing performance is not just about dealing with individuals who are failing to perform. It's also (and perhaps mainly) about enabling performance by providing clear guidelines, policies, frameworks and processes that empower employees to perform at their best. These include continuous performance management, feedback (specifically, 360-degree feedback) and coaching for development.

Continuous performance management

Continuous performance management (CPM): An ongoing process of monitoring, evaluating and improving employee performance in real time rather than waiting for an annual review. It aims to create a dynamic, transparent and collaborative work environment.

Annual performance review: A feedback approach that typically happens once a year and involves an evaluation of performance over the past year against a set of objectives, as well as setting future objectives for the forthcoming year.

While annual performance reviews are still commonly used in organizations, many forward-thinking businesses are shifting towards the more agile practice of continuous performance management (CPM). Annual performance reviews are often criticized for being too time-consuming, ineffective and infrequent.

CPM involves regular check-ins and feedback sessions and, as such, can accommodate shorter-term, more agile goals than traditional annual performance reviews, which only review and set goals once a year. Organizations are generally moving towards more agile working practices, so it makes sense that goal setting should mirror this trend and allow for frequent and meaningful conversations between employees and their managers based on recent events. Some of the benefits of CRM are as follows:

- It aligns employee goals with organizational objectives and allows for timely adjustments to performance and development plans.
- Regular review allows for goals to be adjusted in line with shifting business requirements.
- It helps create a culture of continuous improvement and supports employee engagement, motivation and development. This, in turn, helps to boost retention and minimize staff absences.
- Problems with performance can be spotted as soon as they arise, rather than waiting for the next annual review.
- As it's an ongoing and dynamic process, individuals can see how their short-term efforts align with organizational objectives, which supports motivation.

- Continuously tracking progress provides managers with actionable insights for talent planning.

CPM isn't about continuously moving goal posts or changing what 'good' looks like. It's about engaging the individual and enabling them to thrive and want to produce work or output to their greatest ability. HR can help managers by providing a framework of questions to use in CRM sessions. These questions could focus on both performance and identifying development needs. For example:

- What do you feel went well in your recent project?
- Can you share a recent example where you feel you excelled in your role and were able to play to your key strengths?
- Has anything not gone to plan in recent weeks?
- Can you identify your three main challenges in recent weeks and how you overcame them?
- Can you identify support needs or additional resources that would help you to perform at your best?
- Are there any areas of your work where you feel less confident?
- Do you feel you are meeting the expectations of your role?

Sometimes, a manager may come to you for advice because they have noticed through CPM sessions that an employee is not performing, or that their performance has dipped. These can be difficult conversations for managers, especially for those who are relatively new to the job. A dip in performance often suggests that something has changed, perhaps in the employee's personal circumstances or access to necessary resources at work. Encourage the manager to do the following:

- Clarify expectations so that they are sure the employee knows where their performance is falling short. This might involve reminding the employee of the metrics that are used to measure their performance.

- Explore if something has changed in the employee's personal circumstances.
- Consider any workplace obstacles that might be preventing the employee from performing, for example, a lack of necessary resources or a change in team structure.
- Explore possible solutions, for example, training needs, additional resources or, if the dip in performance is due to poor health, workplace adjustments.

> **Workplace adjustments:** Temporary or permanent changes made by an employer to the workplace or a role to accommodate employees' health conditions and disabilities, and to enable them to continue to do their job.

> **TOP TIP**
> Review your technology
>
> Technology plays a pivotal role in enabling CPM. Digital platforms can facilitate goal setting, tracking and provide real-time feedback by ensuring seamless integration into daily workflows.

> **STOP AND THINK**
>
> How does CPM show up in your organization? If it doesn't, could you introduce it? How can you support managers to have CPM conversations?

Feedback

> **Feedback:** Information given to employees about how they are performing their role, or tasks within their role and the contribution they are making towards achieving organizational goals.

Giving employees regular feedback is important. It boosts their performance and increases overall engagement and motivation. It also helps to identify areas for improvement and possible training and development needs. While managers are predominantly responsible for giving feedback to their teams, HR plays a pivotal role in supporting managers to give effective, fair and consistent feedback by defining feedback processes and methods. In this section, we focus on 360-degree feedback, a method that provides a comprehensive, well-rounded and well-balanced view of someone's strengths and weaknesses.

360-DEGREE FEEDBACK

> **360-degree feedback:** A comprehensive evaluation method where employees receive feedback from various sources, including managers, peers, subordinates, and even clients, to provide a well-rounded view of their performance.

The main objective of 360-degree feedback is to promote personal and professional growth by providing diverse perspectives to empower the individual. Unlike traditional one-way feedback, which flows from a manager to an employee, this approach gathers input from multiple sources. It provides a holistic, well-rounded view of an individual's performance with a focus on strengths, development areas and their overall impact. The feedback process usually involves anonymous surveys or assessments, and the aggregated results are shared with the employee in a manner that enables the employee to reflect and plan their development.

As mentioned earlier in the chapter, traditional annual performance reviews, which were once the cornerstone of workplace feedback, are steadily being phased out by many organizations in favour of CPM. The modern organization has naturally found a replacement that aligns with business agility and employee growth needs. In 360-degree feedback, respondents are often asked to answer questions about employees that relate to the organization's values and behaviours. This enables employees to develop at the same pace as the business, allowing them to remain relevant to the organization's needs and continue working effectively towards achieving organizational goals.

The main advantages of this method are:

- The employee receives input from various perspectives, mitigating bias that might be present when feedback comes from one point of view.
- By cross-referencing multiple viewpoints, individuals gain a clearer understanding of their behaviours and perceptions.
- Peers are encouraged to exchange constructive feedback, leading to better collaboration and strengthening teams. Employees have better insight into each other's strengths and development areas.

TOP TIP
Consider your culture

Feedback can feel threatening if it's not handled respectfully and appropriately. 360-degree feedback works best in organizations with a culture of trust and psychological safety. Psychological safety relates to the feeling that we can speak up and voice our opinions without fear of negative consequences.

STOP AND THINK

Does your organization currently use 360-degree feedback? If so, is it anonymized and processed fairly?

Coaching for development

> **Coaching for development:** A coaching approach that focuses on empowering individuals to grow their skills, improve their performance and reach their personal and professional potential.

Coaching uses open-ended questions that guide an individual to discover their own answers and solutions. The coach acts as a facilitator, rather than an advisor. Among other things, it can involve guiding individuals to:

- Set and pursue specific goals.
- Develop new skills and behaviours.
- Build their confidence and resilience in navigating challenges by recognizing and maximising their unique strengths.

It can take various forms, such as one-on-one sessions, group coaching, or peer coaching. The aim is to empower and provide the tools to employees to take ownership of their development, enhance their skills, and achieve their career aspirations.

Coaching for development is a collaborative process where managers or professional coaches work with employees to set development goals, identify strengths and areas for improvement, and create action plans. It is then the individual's responsibility to follow the steps to attain the identified goal.

> KEY POINT
>
> The fundamental belief of coaching is that the individual has all the knowledge and capability required to achieve their goals, but needs some guidance to uplift them and help them to get there.

Without actionable follow-up, even the most thorough feedback can feel inconsequential. This is where coaching becomes invaluable. By fostering personalized development plans, coaching can turn insights from feedback into actionable growth opportunities for the individual.

While formal executive coaching programmes are well-established, coaching is increasingly becoming accessible across all organizational levels and job roles. Managers and leaders play a crucial role as 'coaches', balancing their traditional supervisory responsibilities with mentoring and development support. Many managers are still not equipped to do this, and it's important that the right training is put in place for this to work effectively. We consider coaching further alongside mentoring in Chapter 5.

STOP AND THINK

Reflect on your own organization of team.

- What types of coaching can you see?
- Are managers trained in providing coaching conversations with their teams?

Sometimes, coaching is very subtle, but ever-present and woven into day-to-day operations. This approach can have a far more significant impact than a formal coaching session.

Salary structures and pay equity

Salary structure: A framework for determining pay in an organization, according to roles, job levels, grades, salary ranges and pay bands.

Pay equity: A concept that ensures fair working practices within a workplace, where employees who perform similar work receive equal pay regardless of their background. It aims to eliminate salary disparities that sometimes arise from discrimination.

HR plays a key role in designing and implementing compensation strategies that attract, motivate and engage employees, leading to improved performance and retention. In Chapter 6, we discuss how salary is, in reality, only one of many things that contribute towards employee engagement, but it is often considered to be a foundational element of engagement and motivation. If it is considered to be unfair, it has the potential to disengage and demotivate employees, leading to poor performance. Compensation is also considered to be a key factor in employee attraction and retention.

Salary structures provide a framework for determining employee compensation. They typically include job grades, salary ranges and pay bands, which are designed to ensure that pay is competitive and aligned with the current market and organizational strategy. Developing a clear and transparent salary structure helps with managing compensation consistently across the organization and promoting fairness in pay decisions.

The three most common types of salary structures are:

- Job-based pay, where compensation is determined by the value of a specific role within the organization.
- Skills-based pay, where compensation is given to employees based on their knowledge, skills and certifications.
- Broadbanding, where compensation or salaries are grouped into fewer, wider pay bands compared to more traditional salary structures. This approach offers flexibility in pay progression and career development by reducing the rigidity of traditional pay scales.

Designing effective salary structures requires striking a balance between internal pay equity (see below) and external competitiveness. Employers must ensure that compensation aligns with both employee contributions and market norms by aligning salaries with industry benchmarks.

There is a growing trend of organizations sharing their salary structures to support transparent and mature conversations. In today's environment, where transparency and equity have become top priorities, salary structures require even greater scrutiny, especially if they are being shared.

Pay equity

Pay equity addresses systemic imbalances in compensation, ensuring that employees performing similar work receive comparable pay, regardless of gender, race or other unrelated factors. It is both a moral and legal imperative, with growing pressure from regulatory bodies, employees and the public. There are some key strategies for achieving pay equity:

- Conducting pay audits through regular analysis of salary data to identify disparities.
- Establishing transparent policies and having clear communication about compensation decisions fosters trust and accountability.
- Eliminating bias by training hiring managers and decision-makers to recognize and mitigate unconscious bias.

Pay equity not only aligns with organizational values but also drives business outcomes. Research consistently shows that diverse, equitable organizations outperform their peers in innovation, employee satisfaction and overall financial performance.

STOP AND THINK

How are salaries structured in your organization? Do you share your salary structure? If not, why do you think that is?

How much focus is there on pay equity? Do you have policies in place, and are hiring managers trained on unconscious bias in relation to pay?

Benefits packages: Health, retirement and perks

While salary is often the headline figure in job offers, the full benefits packages are the unsung heroes of employee compensation. They represent a significant investment by employers and have a profound impact on employee well-being, satisfaction and loyalty.

Benefits can be categorized as follows:

- Heath – benefits such as medical, dental and vision coverage.
- Wellness – initiatives like gym membership, mental health support and nutritional coaching. This can also include health benefits such as preventative care or supplementary health benefits to enhance employee satisfaction.
- Retirement – benefits such as pension plans allow organizations to support their colleagues in their retirement. Responsible organizations care about financial wellbeing. Retirement benefits not only provide peace of mind, but they also foster long-term loyalty, as employees are more likely to remain with employers who invest in their future.
- Perks – these benefits play an increasingly important role in differentiating employers and might include flexible work arrangements such as remote work, flexible hours or unlimited annual leave. They might also include professional development such as course reimbursement, access to online courses or career coaching and lifestyle perks such as company-sponsored events, commuter benefits and discounts on everyday products or services. The key to designing impactful perks is understanding employee preferences. For instance, younger generations often prioritize flexibility and experiences, while others may value job security and stability.

STOP AND THINK

Reflect on your own organization or the team that you work in. How do you currently approach reward and recognition through your benefits package? Is the current design impactful and meeting your employees' expectations? Is it attracting the calibre of new starters that the organization needs?

Linking performance, compensation and benefits

This chapter has considered three crucial elements of HR work that help to attract, engage, motivate and retain employees. While each of these pillars stands on its own, their true strength is in how they interplay. A well-rounded approach ensures that employees feel valued, supported and empowered at every stage of their journey in the organization.

CPM informs compensation decisions by providing real-time data on employee contributions. Pay equity initiatives are closely tied to benefits, as disparities in total compensation often include variations in benefits access or quality. Coaching for development enhances the effectiveness of benefits like professional development programmes, ensuring employees can fully utilize available resources.

As workplaces evolve, so do the challenges and opportunities within these areas. Some key trends include the following:

- Technology integration by using HR tech platforms to streamline feedback, compensation and benefits administration all in one place. This can immediately boost morale.
- Hybrid work considerations, such as adapting salary and benefits to accommodate remote and geographically diverse teams.
- Aligning with employee expectations, which evolve through the generations. For example, Gen Z and Millennials place

greater value on values-driven employment, including equity and wellbeing considerations.

By staying attuned to these trends and continuously innovating, organizations can build a competitive edge while fostering a culture of trust, transparency and excellence. Finally, thoughtfully designed benefits packages address the holistic needs of employees, enhancing loyalty and satisfaction. When these elements align, they create not just a workplace, but a community where individuals and organizations achieve their greatest potential.

KEY POINT

If you currently work for an established global company, you will likely have robust processes, policies and procedures concerning performance, compensation and benefits. The organization will have gone through several growth and maturity stages and will want to attract a diverse workforce. In contrast, many small to medium-sized enterprises may not have this level of rigour, due to the organization's age and not needing to attract a diverse workforce.

WHAT WOULD YOU DO?
Number 4

A manager needs to provide some feedback to a member of their team on their performance. They aren't confident in providing feedback and have asked you how to approach the conversation. How would you advise them to do this?

CHAPTER SUMMARY

- Performance, compensation and benefits are key pillars which allow organizations to navigate the increasingly complex job of attracting and retaining top talent.

- Continuous performance management is a useful and agile tool that allows managers to provide real-time feedback to their employees and address issues as they arise. It has numerous benefits for the employee and employer.

- 360-degree feedback is an effective way to provide holistic feedback to employees, focusing on strengths and development areas. Effective implementation can depend on the organization's culture and psychological safety is a paramount consideration.

- Coaching for development allows employees to set and pursue specific goals that they want to reach and find their own solutions and ways forward.

- Salaries can be structured in numerous ways, including job-based pay, skills-based pay and broadbanding.

- Pay equity ensures that all employees are treated fairly through their compensation and receive comparable pay for similar work.

- Benefits packages can be attractive and motivating. Consider yours carefully to ensure that it aligns with employee expectations and needs.

REVIEW QUESTIONS

1 Write your own definitions of performance, compensation and benefits based on this chapter.

2 Can you name three things that benefit packages typically include apart from salary?

3 Can you describe three ways that performance, compensation and benefits are linked?

CHAPTER FIVE

Learning and development

Introduction

Learning and Development (L&D) is handled differently in different organizations. In larger organizations, it is often a separate department within the HR function, which focuses on designing and implementing training programmes as well as measuring their effectiveness. In smaller organizations, HR generalists may have L&D as part of their remit, and certain L&D responsibilities might be outsourced. The importance of L&D in organizations is often felt most acutely when there is a lack of it available.

This chapter focuses on three core areas of the learning ecosystem: employee training programmes, leadership and succession planning, and career development pathways and programmes.

LEARNING OBJECTIVES

By the end of this chapter, you will be able to:

- Explain what employee training programmes are and why they are important for organizations.

- Understand why choosing a mix of different informal and formal training methods from the learning ecosystem is the most effective approach to L&D.
- Explain the benefits of employee training programmes and the needs that they can address.
- Describe some different coaching can mentoring methods.
- Understand the main components of leadership development and succession planning.
- Articulate the value of career pathways and programmes, and how you can use them to add value to employees and the organization.

Employee training programmes

Employee training programme: Structured plans designed to enhance skills, knowledge and productivity among employees.

Learning ecosystem: The combination of tools, technologies, methods and strategies used to facilitate employee learning and growth.

The primary aim of employee training programmes is to improve performance and boost productivity. Productive employees who are performing at their best feel empowered, engaged and motivated to drive organizational success. Most organizations tailor their employee training programmes to different needs within the organization. For example, in Chapter 4, we looked at the onboarding process and how a key part of this is to provide relevant training to new hires. This might include role-specific training or training on company processes and policies. Other needs that employee training programmes can address include:

- Mandatory training – legally required training or training that is dictated by the organization to ensure that employees meet industry standards and comply with regulations. Unlike other training, this is a non-negotiable component of employment. Topics might include health and safety, compliance, DEI, cybersecurity or customer service training. Onboarding training in company policies and processes is also an example of mandatory training.
- Technical skills – training that focuses on developing employees' capabilities in specific job-related tasks or tools. These are often specialized and industry-specific, including tasks that require proficiency in software, equipment or technical procedures. The importance of technical skills training lies in its ability to help employees remain relevant in a rapidly evolving technological environment and ensure operational efficiency.
- Soft skills – training that focuses on interpersonal skills, emotional intelligence, and behaviours that are crucial for effective communication, teamwork and leadership. Soft skills are universally applicable across industries and play a vital role in building collaborative and productive workplace relationships. Soft skills are sometimes seen as the most important type of skills, as they demonstrate that people can grow and change.

Choosing appropriate training methods

Depending on the size of your organization and budget, you may be able to choose from a range of different training methods to suit different needs. Below is a brief overview of some of the most commonly used methods, which are broadly divided into experiential learning, social learning and formal learning.

A framework commonly used by L&D professionals is the 70:20:10 framework, developed in the 1980s by researchers working at the Center for Creative Leadership. The model suggests that in the workplace, people learn through a range of experiences. 90 per cent of learning happens 'informally' – 70 per cent through on-the-job experiences (otherwise known as experiential learning) and 20 per cent through observing colleagues and social interactions within the workplace (otherwise known as social learning). The further 10 per cent happens through formal training, such as workshops or online training sessions. This emphasizes just how important it is for L&D professionals to consider a range of different learning methods in their employee training programmes.[1]

> **70:20:10 framework:** A learning framework that suggests 70 per cent of learning happens on the job, 20 per cent through interactions and 10 per cent via formal education.

EXPERIENTIAL LEARNING METHODS

You may have learnt about experiential learning in your studies. Experiential learning theory was developed by the psychologist David Kolb in the 1980s. It is basically about learning 'on the job'. The idea is that learning derives from experience and occurs as a four-stage learning cycle:

1 Concrete experience (hands-on practice of a new task, or experience)
2 Reflective observation (reflection of the task and how it was performed deepens the learner's understanding)
3 Abstract conceptualization (the learner adapts their thinking about the task based on their reflection)
4 Active experimentation (the learner applies their adapted thinking to practice when they next have the opportunity to perform the task).[2]

In a workplace scenario, this could look like:

1 A new manager, who has never needed to discuss under-performance with a team member before, meets with an individual about poor performance.

2 After the meeting, the manager reflects on what went well and what could have gone better. They realize that they did all the talking, and perhaps didn't allow the employee sufficient chance to speak and highlight any factors that might be affecting their performance.

3 The manager reframes their thinking about performance discussions to see them as a two-way conversation rather than one-way feedback.

4 The next time the manager discusses underperformance, they approach it differently, ensuring they listen and leaving room for the employee to speak. They learn that the employee is having some health difficulties, and they direct them towards HR colleagues who can help with workplace adjustments. The manager notes the more positive outcome as a result of adjusting their approach.

From an L&D point of view, role-playing training could allow employees to practise difficult conversations such as the above example in a safe environment. Role-playing could also be a useful form of training in the following scenarios:

- Customer service, where employees could practise handling customer complaints.
- Sales, where people could practise their sales techniques and conversations.
- Leadership and management, where, as well as practising performance conversations, people could also hone their conflict resolution skills or interviewing techniques.

An internship is another example of an experiential L&D initiative, where employees enhance their skills and knowledge by gaining practical experience in different roles or departments.

SOCIAL LEARNING METHODS

Social learning is another learning theory that you might be familiar with. It was developed by the psychologist Albert Bandura in the 1950s. The idea behind social learning is that people learn more quickly and effectively in groups as they can exchange knowledge and perspectives. They can see how others act and the consequences of those actions, which quickens the pace of learning. It happens through a process of observing others and imitating their behaviour, which results in acquiring new behaviours, skills and knowledge. With social learning, therefore, knowledge and skills aren't transferred through formal training where the person being trained is a passive recipient of information, but through conversations that happen naturally in the workplace. As such, social learning is therefore a much more informal, but no less effective, type of training.[3]

Social learning is by no means new. It's how humans have learnt from each other since the beginning of time. We are social beings, so this form of learning very much aligns with our natural inclination to connect and share our experiences. Examples of social learning in the workplace could include:

- Observing more experienced employees perform tasks or use some complex software.
- Shadowing or observing mentors or leaders as they solve problems.
- Conversing with a colleague about a new process or system to gain insights.
- Coaching and/or mentoring from more experienced colleagues (more on coaching and mentoring below).
- Collaborating with colleagues either in-person or virtually through online platforms like Teams or Slack.
- Sharing ideas on virtual whiteboards such as Miro.
- Interacting on internal social media networks and discussion forums.

Technology is an important enabler of some social learning. Online platforms, collaborative software, discussion forums, virtual whiteboards and video conferencing can all encourage peer-to-peer interaction and learning.

FORMAL TRAINING METHODS

It may have surprised you to learn that only 10 per cent of learning occurs through formal training methods. It's important to note that there are some who dispute this figure, and it's important to remember that we all have our difference learning styles and preferences.

Formal training is still a very important piece of the L&D puzzle, and the key is to get the mix just right. The fact that formal training only supposedly accounts for 10 per cent of learning doesn't mean that it is not important. In fact, it provides the backbone of any employee training programme because it gives people the theory and factual information that they can then build on in their practice and informal learning. Examples of formal training include structured, instructor-led workshops or training sessions which can happen in-person or online. A lot of the examples of mandatory training we discussed earlier in the chapter would be examples of formal training.

STOP AND THINK

How does your organization blend informal and formal learning methods? Consider the mix between experiential, social and formal training. Can you see any room for improvement, or trying a different approach?

TOP TIP
Create your own course

Consider opportunities to create your own People Management course, which you could deliver to key stakeholders in the organization. It will bring several benefits, including:

- Building your confidence by staying up-to-date with employment legislation and positioning yourself as a trusted advisor.
- Elevating your profile and allowing you to get to know your key stakeholders.
- Developing your presenting skills.

Think about the best way to deliver the training, based on our discussion in the chapter, and what would need to be included. Consider some of the following:

- HR-specific topics such as employee relations, policies and legislation, and equipping people managers for the future of work.
- People-management topics such as leadership styles, emotional intelligence and motivating and engaging your team.
- Practical skills such as conflict resolution, continuous performance management and effective communication.
- Strategic thinking such as decision making, problem solving and managing a dispersed team effectively.
- Workplace dynamics such as change management, health and wellbeing and DEI.

Mentoring and coaching

In this section, we delve a little more deeply into mentoring and coaching, as key components of the learning ecosystem. These provide such a crucial way for employees to learn from others in the organization and grow professionally and personally. This section builds on the discussion in Chapter 4 when we briefly considered coaching as part of managing employee performance.

Mentorship: The process of an experienced member of an organization giving guidance and direction to a less experienced person, known as the 'mentee'.

Reverse mentorship: The process of an experienced member of an organization gaining guidance and direction from a less experienced person to gain new perspectives and insights. In this scenario, the more experienced person is the mentee and the less experienced person is the mentor.

Coaching: A collaborative relationship in which a coach guides a client towards achieving their professional or personal goals and helps them reach their full potential. In contrast to mentorship, a coach does not give direction, but encourages their client to find their own solutions.

Both mentoring and coaching are personalized support systems that provide employees with guidance, feedback, and encouragement to achieve their career goals. While mentorship involves a long-term relationship between a mentor and mentee, coaching is often shorter in duration and focused on specific objectives or skills. Both approaches play a vital role in fostering confidence, refining skills and navigating career challenges.

Reverse mentoring is an interesting idea that gained traction after the former General Electric CEO Jack Welch adopted it in his organization in relation to senior executives learning about emerging technologies from more junior employees. This was in the late 1990s, when the internet was coming into common use. Today, reverse mentoring is often used to help promote DEI, whereby senior executives are mentored by an individual from a marginalized group as well as and digital literacy in organizations.

Key theories related to mentoring and coaching to be aware of include:

- Transformational coaching – where a coach inspires and challenges mentees to grow beyond their current capabilities to support colleagues to fulfil their full potential and provide a boost in performance.

- GROW coaching model – this acronym stands for 'Goal' (what the person wants to achieve), 'Reality' (the current situation verses the goal and an assessment of the facts and challenges that might lie ahead), 'Options' (the coach helps the coachee to assess different solutions through brainstorming) and 'Way forward' (the action plan).
- Cognitive apprenticeship – where a mentor (or other experienced person) teaches skills or imparts knowledge to an apprentice (or less experienced person). The guidance given by the mentor reduces over time as the mentee gains experience.

TOP TIP
Participate in mentoring yourself

As you progress in your career, aim to always have a mentor or to mentor someone else. It will increase your confidence, improve your communication skills and help you to progress more quickly.

Leadership development and succession planning

Another key element of L&D's remit is to identify and help develop future leaders in the organization and put robust succession plans in place. We briefly considered succession programmes in Chapter 3 in the context of sourcing candidates for roles and we consider it further below.

Leadership development and succession planning are two sides of the same coin, integral to the sustainable growth, stability and adaptability of organizations. Together, they create a robust framework for fostering talent, maintaining stability and adaptability and driving long-term growth.

Leadership development: The process of enhancing the skills, knowledge and attributes of current and future leaders in the organization.

> **Succession planning:** The process of ensuring the continuity of leadership within an organization.

Leadership development

Leadership development is the process of enhancing the skills, knowledge, and attributes of individuals to enable them to take on leadership roles effectively. This development is not confined to managerial levels but can also apply to employees at different levels who show potential leadership qualities. Leadership development is crucial as it equips individuals to navigate challenges, inspire teams, drive innovation, and achieve organizational objectives. Leadership is a key driver of success for any organization so it's important to get this right for the future stability of the organization. Leadership development might include, but not be limited to, the following key topics:

- Navigating challenges.
- Inspiring teams.
- Driving innovation.
- Resolving conflicts.
- Managing change.
- Making effective decisions.
- Managing difficult conversations.
- Achieving organizational objectives.

In the modern business landscape, rapid change and globalization are common, so leadership development is more important than ever. Organizations need leaders who can adapt to evolving circumstances, foster a positive work environment, and align their teams with organizational goals for continued prosperity.

TRAINING NEEDS ANALYSIS FOR LEADERSHIP

So how do you figure out the best approach or areas of focus for leadership development for each individual or cohorts within your organization? The best way is to do a training needs analysis (TNA), which aligns leadership development with broader organizational goals, so that you can be sure the investment in training will be worthwhile. A TNA seeks to identify the skills, knowledge and competencies that individuals or cohorts need training in so that an organization can reach its goals. It tends to have a long-term outlook and consider future training needs as well as immediate ones.

> **Training needs analysis (TNA):** The process of analysing the current skills, knowledge and competencies of employees and comparing them to the skills, knowledge and competencies necessary for them to perform their roles well and contribute towards organizational goals. The gap between the two represents the training needs.

We don't have enough room in this chapter to consider TNA in detail, but the basic steps are as follows:

1. Define your objectives
This involves considering your organizational goals and defining what you aim to achieve through leadership training. Ultimately, you want to identify areas where individuals or cohorts may need training to achieve organizational goals. Consider the following broad examples of organizational goals:

- Increase sales.
- Improve employee engagement.
- Improve customer satisfaction score.

The first step would be to identify the skills, knowledge and competencies that leaders would need to achieve these goals. Not all goals will be applicable to all leaders. For example, the goal 'improve employee engagement' is relevant to all leaders across the organization, 'increase sales' is likely to be relevant to a smaller cohort – perhaps just those in sales and marketing.

2. Assess current skills, knowledge and competencies of leaders in the organization in relation to these goals

You can use performance data as your starting point (refer to Chapter 4), but this might not give you enough information to thoroughly assess the current levels to identify training needs. You could also consider collecting data through observations, surveys and interviews.

3. Identify skills, knowledge and competency gaps

Compare the current skills, knowledge and competencies with the required skills, knowledge and competencies and identify gaps that training could address.

4. Prioritize training needs based on their impact on organizational goals

After performing the above, you will be in a good position to define the organization's training needs for leadership development and develop a training plan.

Succession planning

Succession planning is the proactive process of identifying and developing future leaders to fill key positions within an organization. The objective is to ensure a smooth leadership transition in the event of retirements, resignations or sudden leadership changes so that organizations can continue to work towards their goals. Succession planning is vital as it minimizes disruptions and maintains operational continuity while fostering a culture of internal talent growth. This is key to maintaining productivity in organizations.

A lack of succession planning can leave an organization vulnerable, particularly during times of leadership change. A well-thought-out plan ensures the longevity of the organization, ensuring it is well-equipped to deal with future challenges, and maintains stakeholder confidence.

THE NINE-BOX GRID

A tool that you could look to explore and introduce in your organization is the nine-box grid, which helps organizations evaluate employee performance and potential and combine the two to identify future leaders, as well as their development needs. The grid consists of nine boxes in a 3×3 matrix. The X (horizontal) axis shows an individual's current performance, based on their KPIs, one-to-ones and performance development reviews. The Y (vertical) axis represents their potential to grow into more complex roles or leadership positions. Individuals can then be plotted on this grid according to their performance and potential:

- Those with high performance and potential are immediately identifiable as future leaders who might be able to step into leadership roles fairly soon.
- Those with medium performance and medium or high potential or high performance and medium potential could be identified as being able to step into leadership roles eventually, but over a longer time horizon than the high potentials and high performers.

TOP TIP
Hone your coaching skills

As an HR professional, you play a key role in leadership development as you will most likely be the one who is coaching leaders. Of course, some organizations use external organizations to deliver this service, but it would be useful to always have the capability to do this yourself if you can. It helps bring the value of HR to the organization, and, most importantly, the value you bring to your role.

Career development pathways and programmes

Career development pathway: A roadmap for employees outlining how they can progress in the organization through specific roles.

Career development programme: A structured initiative aimed at providing employees with tools, resources and training to advance their skills, knowledge and competencies and prepare them for future roles.

Upskilling: The process of training employees to enhance their existing skills for career growth.

Reskilling: The process of teaching employees new skills so they can transition into different roles.

Career development pathways and programmes are transformative tools for employees and employers. They provide employees with structured opportunities for growth and empower them to unlock their potential, while ensuring organizations remain competitive and resilient in changing markets. By investing in career development programmes and mentorship initiatives, companies create a foundation for long-term success, innovation and employee satisfaction.

Pathways and programmes are slightly different:

- Pathways provides a roadmap to show how an employee can progress through an organization and their potential future roles.

- Programmes are structured initiatives that aim to upskill and reskill employees and develop their knowledge and competencies to prepare them for future roles. They are therefore a fundamental part of, and often directly contribute to, career development pathways.

Many career development pathways and programmes include personalized mentoring and coaching as a core component, which we discussed earlier in the chapter. A pathway might include it as a specific stage or milestone that an individual would need to complete to progress within the organization, whereas a programme might include it as a component to help employees develop new skills.

Career development pathways are designed to help individuals navigate their personal professional growth while also ensuring organizations build a competent, future-ready workforce. They empower individuals to identify their goals, acquire necessary skills, and ultimately achieve their aspirations. As an HR professional, you will be involved in the background work. For example, you will look at the job profiles and work with the area or business unit to look at what roles are needed, and what structured pathways to devise to support the necessary infrastructure.

Career development programmes are structured initiatives aimed at providing employees with the tools, resources and opportunities to advance their careers. These programmes enable individuals to align their professional ambitions with organizational objectives. They are a cornerstone of employee engagement and retention strategies (refer to Chapter 6), as employees value opportunities to grow and progress within their workplace. As an HR professional, you will devise and facilitate career development programmes, so it's important you are aware of all the free and paid for resources available in your organization. This will help you to act as a strategic partner to the organization to link the right individuals with the available resources. By connecting the dots, you can enable people's dreams, passions and careers.

TOP TIP

Continuously review your career development programmes

Needs and demands change and evolve. There are currently five generations in the workplace who all have very different needs. As an HR professional it's important to ensure that the right programmes are in place for continuous improvement and continuous growth to support the ongoing needs of the organization you work for.

Key theories to be aware of in this area of HR work include:

- Holland's career typology theory – this suggests that people choose careers based on personality types, and that their career paths align with their strengths and interests.[4]
- Krumboltz's social learning theory of career decision making – this suggests that career choices are influenced by learning experiences, environmental factors and personal beliefs. Organizations can support this approach by providing exposure to different roles through job rotations.[5]
- Protean career theory – over the years protean career theory has become more popular as it looks at employees taking ownership of their career paths and adapting to changes in the job market. Organizations can encourage self-directed learning and flexible career progression.
- Boundaryless career theory – this theory suggests that careers are not confined to single organizations or industries, and that employees develop transferable skills through cross-functional experiences that organizations can support.

STOP AND THINK

Are there good opportunities for career advancement in your organization? Do you use career development pathways and programmes and mentorship and coaching to help employees progress throughout the organization according to their strengths and interests?

TOP TIP
Engage your people managers

L&D is more than just providing online training modules. It's about finding out what each individual needs to be able to thrive in their role. Consider holding people management workshops for all leaders in your organization, including your executive team. This enables you to build key relationships through demonstrating your knowledge and the value you bring to your role and organization. Refer back to Chapter 2 where we discussed storytelling to help you deliver impact.

WHAT WOULD YOU DO?
Number 5

A senior manager comes to you as they have an issue with their workforce planning and need help to identify their top talent. How would you advise them, and what steps would you take?

CHAPTER SUMMARY

- Employee training programmes are essential investments for individuals and organizations. They equip employees with the tools to excel in their roles and foster a culture of continuous learning and improvement.

- Employee training programmes are designed to enhance the skills, knowledge and productivity among employees. They can comprise experiential learning (learning on the job), social learning (learning through observing and interactions with colleagues) and formal learning, such as instructor-led workshops.

- Mentoring and coaching are a key part of the learning ecosystem and can be incorporated into employee development pathways and programmes.

- A key part of L&D's remit is to identify future leaders in the organization and put robust succession plans into place so that the organization can continue meeting its goals over time.

- Investing in career development pathways and programmes sets organizations up for long-term success and increases employee engagement and retention.

REVIEW QUESTIONS

1 Name three reasons why L&D is important for employees and their organizations.

2 Why is it important to mix experiential, social and formal learning methods?

3 What's the difference between a development pathway and development programme?

Endnotes

1 Cloke, H (2024) The 70:20:10 model: A guide to optimizing your training strategy, Growth Engineering Technologies, 9 February, https://www.growthengineering.co.uk/70-20-10-model (archived at https://perma.cc/XEL4-5M5W)

2 Practera (nd) Become involved in experiential learning, https://practera.com/what-is-the-experiential-learning-theory-of-david-kolb (archived at https://perma.cc/GA6G-T5W9)

3   Koumparaki, E (2024) Social learning: Benefits and use in the workplace and L&D, talentlms, 9 April, https://www.talentlms.com/blog/social-learning-in-elearning/# (archived at https://perma.cc/SM7R-QXBD)

4   Career Key (nd) Holland's theory of career choice and you, www.careerkey.org/fit/personality/hollands-theory-of-career-choice (archived at https://perma.cc/7DEJ-Z6R4)

5   Yunus, N et al (2024) Understanding career decision-making: Influencing factors and application of Krumboltz's social learning theory, *International Journal of Academic Research in Business and Social Sciences*, 4 July, https://hrmars.com/papers_submitted/21562/understanding-career-decision-making-influencing-factors-and-application-of-krumboltzs-social-learning-theory.pdf (archived at https://perma.cc/5NX5-QUVU)

CHAPTER SIX

Employee engagement and retention

Introduction

Employee engagement and retention are two of the most critical aspects of HRM. They play a crucial role in shaping a company's success by ensuring that employees are committed to their work and remain with the organization for an extended period. Employee engagement is the foundation of a thriving and resilient organization and workforce. Engaged employees are happy, motivated and likely to stay with the organization over the long term, contributing towards its ongoing success.

This chapter continues the discussion of many themes introduced in previous chapters to show how they relate to employee engagement, such as compensation and benefits and having the opportunity to develop and progress within an organization. We start by looking at what employee engagement and retention are, explaining why employee engagement is important for organizations and how it contributes to retention. We then examine the key drivers of engagement, ranging from intrinsic motivators such as purpose and autonomy to extrinsic factors like rewards and recognition. Understanding these drivers enables organizations to tailor their strategies and foster an engaged workforce.

We then look at HR's role in employee engagement, which centres around measuring it to understand engagement levels and patterns and putting strategies into place to improve it. As part of measuring engagement, we take an in-depth look at employee surveys, as this is the main method used by organizations. We end the chapter by looking at the importance of building a positive organizational culture to foster employee engagement.

LEARNING OBJECTIVES

By the end of this chapter, you will be able to:

- Define employee engagement and explain how it has evolved.
- Explain why employee engagement is important.
- Explain the main drivers of employee engagement.
- Explain ways to measure engagement to understand levels in your organization, including through employee surveys.
- Provide your own definition of organizational culture and understand its importance in maintaining an engaged workforce.

What are employee engagement and retention?

Employee engagement: A term that describes how an individual feels about their work and employer, including their level of enthusiasm, the degree to which they feel connected and involved with their work, and their motivation to perform well.

Employee retention: An organization's ability to keep its employees over an extended period by implementing strategies to build a positive organizational culture and work environment.

Employee engagement is often understood to mean how an employee feels about their work and the organization they work for. It refers to the level of emotional commitment and dedication an employee applies to their organization and its goals. It is an emotional and psychological state which is reflected in the work that people do. Engaged employees are generally considered to be enthusiastic, happy and productive employees and prepared to go 'above and beyond' to contribute positively towards their organization's success. They are also less likely to call in sick or have long spells of absence. It therefore follows that engaged employees are more likely to stay with their organization for longer. This is why engagement is considered to be a key factor in reducing employee turnover over time.

There is no single, unifying definition of employee engagement. The original concept is often attributed to the organizational psychologist William Kahn, who first proposed it in the 1990s after studying workplace behaviour. He identified three interconnected psychological conditions that are necessary for employees to 'express themselves physically, cognitively and emotionally' at work:

1 Meaningfulness – if an employee finds their work meaningful, they understand how it adds value to the organization or society, and feel it is worthwhile giving their full self to their work.
2 Safety – employees need to feel safe and secure to be able to fully express themselves and be themselves at work.
3 Availability – available employees have the physical and emotional resources to engage fully with their work.[1]

Kahn's findings are similar to those from research carried out by Richard Ryan and Edward Deci at the University of Rochester in 1985. Ryan and Deci proposed a theory of human motivation called self-determination theory. It states that people feel motivated when three psychological needs are met:

1 Autonomy – this relates to the need to have the freedom to make decisions and feel in control of your work.
2 Competence – relates to feeling sufficiently capable and skilled to perform the task at hand.
3 Relatedness – relates to the need to feel connected to people (or colleagues, in the workplace) and part of a larger organization.[2]

Earlier, in the late 1950s, the psychologist Frederick Herzberg had proposed his two-factor theory to provide an understanding of what motivates us:

1 Motivators – these factors are related to workplace satisfaction. They include achievement, recognition and opportunities to progress within the organization.
2 Hygiene – these factors prevent dissatisfaction but don't inherently motivate people. They include salary, benefits and working conditions.[3]

We'll draw on these ideas throughout this chapter. While the concept of motivation is not exactly the same as engagement, the two ideas are very closely linked. Motivation is generally considered to be an internal state that makes humans act in a certain way. Ryan and Deci distinguished between two types of motivation – intrinsic and extrinsic. They defined intrinsic motivation as the drive to act because we are interested in the activity, or it makes us feel fulfilled. They defined extrinsic motivation as the role that external factors, such as pay and reward and recognition, have on our drive to act or behave in a certain way. The idea of intrinsic and extrinsic motivating factors is closely linked to some of the drivers of engagement that we consider later in the chapter.

> **Intrinsic motivation:** The desire to act based on internal drivers such as interest, passion or fulfilment.

Extrinsic motivation: The desire to act based on external factors such as pay and reward.

Gallup's employee engagement survey

Gallup is a global analytics and advisory firm that has measured employee engagement using its Q12 survey since the early 2000s. This survey assesses employee engagement consistently through 12 questions, ranging from basic needs, such as how satisfied employees are with their company and whether they know what is expected of them, through to questions seeking to learn how appreciated people feel at work, whether their opinions count, they have a best friend at work, feel aligned with their organization's purpose and have sufficient opportunities to develop and grow. You can see that these questions draw on ideas from Kahn's and Ryan and Deci's research.

TOP TIP
Visit Gallup's website

Gallup's Q12 survey is a great modern tool that you can adapt to your organization depending on your needs. Visit their website to find the list of questions.

Several factors drive employee engagement. These are important for HR professionals to understand if they are to be effective in improving engagement levels, which we discuss later in the chapter.

Drivers of employee engagement

Gallup believes that five factors drive engagement:

- The ability to derive meaning and purpose from work.
- Development opportunities.
- A caring manager who can coach employees to improve.
- Ongoing conversations.
- A focus on employees' strengths rather than weaknesses.[4]

While it's useful to have this focus from Gallup, there are, in fact, many other factors that can also be considered to drive engagement. We now consider Gallup's factors, alongside some others.

Meaningful work

Gallup's top point is that people feel engaged if they derive meaning and purpose from their work. It increases job satisfaction and motivation. This can be a tricky thing for organizations to influence, as a sense of purpose is very personal. What feels purposeful to me might not necessarily feel purposeful to you. However, organizations can help to foster a sense of purpose and meaning by clearly communicating their own purpose and mission in their values and employer branding. In Chapter 3, we briefly discussed Benjamin Schneider's Attraction-Selection-Attrition framework, which states that organizations tend to attract, select and retain individuals who align with their values, culture and mission. The same is true for purpose – if an organization clearly states its purpose in its employer branding, it will be more likely to attract like-minded individuals who will be able to find a sense of purpose in their work, should they progress to become an employee.

Effective leadership and management

Gallup states that having a caring manager is an important driver of engagement. Management and leadership have an important role to play in employee engagement. Managers are in daily contact with their teams, and if they are not engaged themselves, it is unlikely that they will be able to engage their team. An engaged manager cares about their team and wants them to do well. They build strong relationships with team members and provide regular feedback, recognizing individuals' contributions and fostering a positive working environment (refer to the discussion in Chapter 4).

Effective leadership is also important. Leaders who communicate a clear vision, provide guidance and inspire their teams can significantly influence engagement levels.

Two-way communication and the employee voice

Communicating with and actively listening to employees' concerns and suggestions is a powerful driver of engagement. The mechanisms an organization provides to allow employees to voice their views and opinions are known as 'employee voice'. It can include things like informal feedback from employee to employer and more formal communication channels such as focus groups. Employee voice aims to foster a culture in which employees feel they have a say in how things are done in their workplace. It ties in with Gallup's point about ongoing conversations. Employees feel heard, and it helps to build trust between employees and their managers. We consider this important point in more detail later in the chapter.

Flexible and hybrid work

Organizations that promote flexible working arrangements by offering remote work options and respecting employees' personal time contribute to higher engagement levels. When employees feel that their personal lives are valued, they are more likely to be committed and engaged in their work.

Career development and growth

As discussed in Chapter 5, career development and growth within an organization create an engaged workforce. This is done by providing training programmes, mentoring, coaching and clear career progression paths as employees feel invested in and remain loyal to the organization. This ties in with Gallup's point about focusing on employees' strengths. If employees can forge a career path through the organization where they can use their natural talents and abilities, they will feel more confident and engaged.

Adequate resources and tools

Providing employees with the necessary resources, technology and tools to do their jobs well is crucial for engagement. Having what you need to do your job means you can be effective, productive and it increases job satisfaction.

Pay and reward

We covered pay and benefits in Chapter 4. In the past, pay and benefits were considered by many to be the primary drivers of engagement, but we now know that intrinsic factors are often more motivating than extrinsic ones like pay. This does not, however, mean that pay can be overlooked. As discussed in Chapter 4, if organizations want to attract top talent, they need competitive pay packages. Think of pay as the foundation. If it's too low, it's likely to demotivate and disengage employees. But if pay is fair, many people's engagement levels will be more driven by intrinsic factors. That being said, some people are very engaged by the opportunity to enhance their pay through things like bonuses.

> **STOP AND THINK**
>
> How much does your organization consider these engagement drivers? Is there evidence in your organization of employees' roles being aligned with their strengths and interests? Do employees understand how their work contributes towards organizational goals?

Measuring and improving engagement

As an HR professional, your role in employee engagement is likely to be:

1 Understanding engagement levels in your organization by measuring them.
2 Devising strategies, policies and putting plans into place to improve engagement levels in your organization.

Measuring engagement

The first point relates to understanding engagement through gathering employee feedback and perspectives on their job and the organization. This can be done via a range of quantitative and qualitative methods, such as:

- Employee surveys (we consider these in detail below).
- Tracking metrics such as turnover, absenteeism, productivity and employee net promoter score (eNPS).
- Employee interviews and focus groups (we consider these in detail below).

The employee survey is the most common way of seeking feedback from employees and can include both quantitative questions, which seek numerical responses from employees, for example, asking them to rate something on a specific scale and qualitative, open-ended questions that ask employees to expand on their answers so that you can gain a more nuanced understanding of their perspectives. We'll go on to consider this now.

> **Quantitative feedback:** Numerical data that can be used to spot trends and patterns.

> **Qualitative feedback:** Data in the form of words or observations that allows for a more nuanced understanding of the research topic.

> **Employee net promoter score (eNPS):** A metric that tracks how likely employees are to recommend their organization as a good place to work.

> **Employee surveys:** A questionnaire designed to gather information to evaluate morale, engagement, achievement and overall employee satisfaction.

EMPLOYEE SURVEYS

We'll now delve a little more into the importance of employee voice, specifically, enabling employee feedback through employee surveys and other feedback mechanisms.

Organizations need to foster a feedback culture where employees feel safe and encouraged to give and receive feedback. Employee surveys and feedback mechanisms are tools for understanding employee engagement and identifying areas that are working well and areas for improvement. They provide valuable insights into perceptions, satisfaction levels and suggestions to enhance the working environment.

There are several types of surveys you could use to gather employee feedback:

- Engagement surveys measure motivation, commitment and morale.
- Satisfaction surveys assess how satisfied employees are with various aspects of their role.
- Pulse surveys are short, frequent surveys that can be used as a 'temperature test' in real time.
- Exit surveys are used to collect insights from employees leaving the organization which can be used to make improvements for future and current employees.
- Onboarding surveys help you understand new hires' experiences of those crucial early days with the organization

(refer to Chapter 3). They provide insights into what works well and what improvements can be made.

Surveys provide a real-time snapshot of the current feeling in the organization. They are incredibly valuable for 'taking the temperature' at certain points and should be done regularly (rather than annually) to maximize employee engagement.

Questions can vary from job satisfaction, work-life balance, leadership, communication or overall organizational culture. Using a mix of quantitative and qualitative questions can provide a comprehensive view of employees' experiences. Earlier in the chapter, we considered Herzberg's two-factor theory as a way to understand human motivation. Employee surveys should assess both motivating and hygiene factors to improve employee satisfaction. As a reminder, hygiene factors are necessary to prevent employees from feeling dissatisfied and disengaged, but they don't inherently motivate people.

TOP TIP
Get your survey schedule right

While it's important to use surveys regularly, it's also very important not to bombard employees with surveys, especially those that are overly long or complex, as it can result in survey fatigue. Survey fatigue happens when employees are asked to complete surveys too frequently. It results in lower response rates, rushed responses and an overall reduction in the quality of the data.

There is real value in ensuring anonymity and confidentiality, as this provides a foundation for honest feedback. Employees are more likely to share their true feelings and concerns if they know their identities are protected.

> **TOP TIP**
> Consider a third-party survey platform
>
> Many organizations use third-party survey platforms with robust privacy measures to guarantee anonymity, as it can make a real difference to employee response rates and how honest they feel they can be in their feedback.

Once you have the survey results, it's important to analyse the data and identify key themes and areas for improvement, as this drives change and, by extension, employee engagement. Employees will soon get survey fatigue if they feel their responses are not being acted on. Taking action demonstrates a commitment to employees, builds trust and credibility and encourages further participation in future surveys.

OTHER FEEDBACK MECHANISMS

Other feedback channels organizations could incorporate include:

- Suggestion boxes or schemes – this is a traditional method which allows employees to give feedback anonymously. They can provide insight into barriers people might be experiencing, for example, if they lack the necessary tools and resources to do their job well. Suggestion boxes can be physical or online.
- Focus groups – in-person or online focus groups can provide employees with the opportunity to share detailed insights and perspectives into specific issues.
- One-to-one meetings between managers and employees – these provide a more informal way for employees to share feedback. This relates to the point made earlier in the chapter about the importance of having a caring and supportive manager. Caring managers will act on feedback. If an employee shares feedback with a manager and it is not acted

upon, this is likely to disengage the employee. Some managers may need support from HR in this aspect of their work.

TOP TIP
Consider recognizing employees for their feedback

Recognizing employees who provide valuable feedback can encourage continued participation in feedback mechanisms. Encourage managers to acknowledge their contributions, publicly or privately. Recognition could range from verbal praise to company-wide acknowledgement.

STOP AND THINK

How does your organization currently measure employee engagement? Can you list three ways, and can you identify any suggestions you could make to improve how they measure it, based on this chapter?

How do you personally measure employee engagement – through gut feel, culture or metrics?

Improving engagement

HR's role in improving engagement is closely linked to improving culture, which we discuss later in the chapter. In reality, HR professionals cannot improve engagement or culture alone, but they can instigate a range of activities or initiatives that can be put in place throughout the organization. This also isn't something that can happen overnight. Improving engagement levels and culture requires a long-term strategy and leadership buy-in. Examples of ways to improve engagement include, but are not limited to:

- Learning and development initiatives (refer to our discussion in Chapter 5).

- Recognition schemes to acknowledge effort and achievement in different ways. These could include one-on-one praise, public praise (perhaps in the form of 'employee of the month' awards) or monetary recognition such as pay rises and bonuses.
- Clear career development pathways and programmes (refer to Chapter 5).
- Mentoring and coaching schemes.

Most importantly, HR can help to improve engagement by engaging with managers and leaders who interact with their teams on a day-to-day basis. How you work with managers to help them resolve conflicts, provide effective feedback or coach their teams all feeds into fostering a positive work culture that engages employees. You can do this by identifying managers' training needs, making sure they have access to the policies, tools and templates they need and holding them accountable for their teams' engagement through metrics and feedback.

Ultimately, the most effective way to improve engagement over time is to build a positive organizational culture. We'll end this chapter by considering the importance of culture and what HR professionals can do to help change it.

TOP TIP

Check the open-ended questions

Check your employee engagement survey, if you have one, for suggestions on how you could improve engagement levels. You are likely to find this in the answers to qualitative questions, where employees can give more detailed answers. These suggestions will be specific to your own context and culture, and might be more effective than implementing more generalized approaches.

Building a positive organizational culture

Positive organizational culture: A culture in which employees feel engaged, valued and motivated so that they can thrive and be the best versions of themselves.

All organizations have a culture, but it's not always a good one. Bad cultures are sometimes referred to as 'toxic'. They can be marred by internal politics, dysfunctional behaviours and poor communication. A positive, or good, employee culture is the opposite. Employee wellbeing is prioritized, there is open communication between the employer and employees, people trust each other and they therefore thrive in their work. The CIPD describes a positive organizational culture as one that 'allows employees to understand their organization and feel that their voice matters in driving the business towards a common purpose'.[5]

Culture evolves over time, and it is often allowed to do so without any intervention, which is how organizations can end up with unhelpful and toxic cultures. Fostering a positive organizational culture is possible by taking a proactive and strategic approach. This is sometimes seen as HR's role, or that HR has ownership of 'culture' within an organization. This is a misconception. In reality, creating a positive culture is ultimately leadership's responsibility, and it starts with the CEO, although it involves a concerted effort from leaders and employees alike. HR professionals can support and advise on strategies to improve culture through their work with leaders in the organization.

A positive employee culture prioritizes employee wellbeing. Building a positive culture is linked to supporting employees' wellbeing through providing a wellness programme, mental health support and initiatives that promote work-life balance, all of which can improve overall employee satisfaction. Employee wellbeing should be a priority in creating a positive culture, as it can prevent employees from becoming burnt out, which creates high levels of absence and impacts productivity and output.

Creating an inclusive culture

The CIPD emphasizes the need to build inclusive workplace cultures. A positive organizational culture embraces and celebrates diverse perspectives and creates an inclusive environment where all employees feel valued and respected. Organizations that build a culture of acceptance and belonging also foster innovation and engagement, as diverse perspectives can challenge the kind of 'groupthink' that stagnates an organization. Organizations that innovate are in a better position to compete and are more likely to succeed in their market, which further adds to the argument for creating inclusive cultures.

> **Groupthink:** A way of thinking that groups of people fall into, where they all think along the same or similar lines to conform and avoid disagreements. It's dangerous as it doesn't allow for critical or innovative thinking and differing perspectives.

> **TOP TIP**
> Work with senior leaders to develop culture
>
> While you are unlikely to work directly with the CEO as an early career professional, you are likely to partner with senior leaders in your organization. Think about how you can effectively partner with leaders in your area or remit and coach them on how to develop a positive organization culture.

Kotter's change model

Changing organizational culture is not easy, and there's no quick fix. People often use John P Kotter's 8-step change model to manage cultural change, which he developed in the mid-1990s.

It outlines a structured and top-down approach to initiating, implementing and sustaining cultural change. At the heart of Kotter's model is the idea that change is about emotion and momentum, not just processes and systems. It provides a clear, linear roadmap to help organizations shift their culture:

1 Establish urgency for change – this involves demonstrating why change is necessary and why doing nothing is not an option.
2 Build a guiding coalition – create an influential team that can champion the change throughout the organization.
3 Develop a vision and strategy – change needs a future vision which outlines where you want to get to and aligns everyone around a common goal.
4 Enlist a volunteer army – create a large group of people in the organization who feel passionately about the change and will act as ambassadors for it in the organization.
5 Enable action by removing barriers – this is when you empower employees to take action and remove any obstacles. An example of an obstacle might be employee resistance to change. Organizations can address this by communicating more with employees, focusing on engaging them further and explaining why change is necessary.
6 Generate short-term wins – this aims to build momentum and increase buy-in. The idea is to provide evidence that the change is working.
7 Sustain acceleration – here, you build on early wins and scale changes across the organization.
8 Institute change – this involves anchoring new approaches to the culture within the organization. It's about embedding the change and making it a permanent part of how things are done.[6]

The CIPD recommends avoiding fanfare when it comes to initiating cultural change. It suggests that a low-key approach and small changes are more likely to be effective than announcing it officially. It also agrees with Kotter that conveying the vision and need for change to the wider organization is a vital first step.

Building a positive organizational culture that fosters engagement can be done through some of the drivers of engagement discussed earlier in the chapter, such as having a caring manager, employee voice and being flexible about where and when you allow employees to work. Through continuous learning, organizations can encourage employees to pursue professional development opportunities, attend workshops and engage in skill-building activities. This demonstrates the organization's commitment to employee personal and professional growth.

Celebrating success and milestones, no matter how big or small, reinforces positive culture. It provides recognition for individual and team achievements, and through acknowledging employees' contributions, it creates a sense of pride and accomplishment.

Fostering teamwork is also a simple way of creating a sense of community and encouraging a culture of collaboration. As an HR professional, work with managers to create opportunities for employees to work together on projects, share ideas and support one another. Cross-functional initiatives can further enhance collaboration and enable the organization to leverage shared experience.

Crucially, an organization's core values and mission are at the heart of its culture, so this is a good place to start when assessing culture and identifying areas that might need to change.

TOP TIP
Involve your CEO

As an HR professional, why not think about how your CEO can directly thank or reward individual contributors or teams on successful projects?

> **STOP AND THINK**
>
> Return to the drivers of engagement we considered earlier in the chapter and consider them in the context of your own organization. How does your organization use each driver to improve the culture in the organization? Can you identify anything that could be done differently?

The organization's core values and mission

> **Values:** A set of core beliefs that state what an organization stands for. Values aim to reflect and shape an organization's culture.

> **Mission:** A statement that defines an organization's purpose – why it exists – and how it serves its stakeholders.

We briefly considered organizational values earlier in the chapter concerning meaningful work and in Chapter 3 concerning employer branding and candidate attraction. An organization's values and purpose form the foundation of its culture, but this is often forgotten in the day-to-day management of the organization, especially during busy periods. In an ideal world, they should direct culture by providing a set of principles for all employees to follow. In reality, this often doesn't happen, as organizations fail to make their values sufficiently visible by communicating them consistently and embedding them in hearts and minds.

Leaders should embody the organization's values to set the tone for the rest of the organization. For example, if hybrid or flexible working is important to the organization's culture, employees should see their leaders working from home, or leaving at an agreed time before the end of the typical working day to pick up their children.

STOP AND THINK

Reflect on your organization's own values and purpose, using the following questions to help you:

- How effectively do the leaders in your organization embody your values? Do they prioritize their wellbeing and demonstrate ethical behaviour, for example?

- How often does your organization communicate its values to employees? Are they reinforced at key points, such as in group meetings and performance reviews?

- Does your organization recognize employees who consistently demonstrate values in their behaviour and work?

- Does your organization reinforce its values through events and initiatives?

Your role as an HR professional

As an HR professional, you can help to embed organizational values by doing the following:

- Clearly and consistently communicating values across all touchpoints of the employee experience (for example, in recruitment, onboarding, performance reviews, surveys and exit surveys) so that employees are in no doubt about what the organization stands for.
- Finding ways to involve employees in shaping or refining core values to increase buy-in, for example, through focus groups.
- Aligning HR policies and procedures with organizational values. To do this, start by defining how the values translate into expected practices and behaviours, and review your policies and procedures to assess alignment.

- Spend time with leaders in your area and their teams and coach them in how to improve their cultures and align them more with organizational values.

CASE STUDY
How HR can help to increase engagement

Imagine the following scenario:

An organization is facing an annual turnover rate of 22 per cent in critical technical roles, with engagement scores showing low trust in leadership, poor communication and unclear career paths. The HR team develop a three-part strategy:

1 Leadership visibility through monthly all-hands meetings with transparent updates from senior leaders.

2 Career growth and development by launching a structured career framework for engineers. Progression doesn't necessarily mean being a manager – individuals can progress as sole contributors.

3 Provision of wellbeing initiatives such as mental health resources and flexible work arrangements.

WHAT WOULD YOU DO?
Number 6

You have started to partner with a new area director. Employee engagement metrics show that their area's morale has been in decline for several years. You have been asked to think of some ideas to share with the director that they could implement to boost morale. What would you suggest?

CHAPTER SUMMARY

- Employee engagement is a term that refers to how an employee feels about their work and how committed they feel towards helping the organization reach its goals.

- High employee engagement reduces turnover and contributes towards the successful retention of employees over time.

- There are several drivers of engagement, which can be broadly understood in terms of intrinsic and extrinsic motivators. Pay and reward are extrinsic motivators. While perhaps not as powerful as intrinsic motivators, they may demotivate people if they are unfair.

- HR professionals contribute towards employee engagement by measuring it to understand levels and patterns over time and putting strategies into place to improve it.

- The employee survey is perhaps the most common method for understanding engagement levels in an organization.

- Building a positive organizational culture takes time, and commitment needs to come from the top. It starts with defining organizational values, ensuring that leaders embody them and aligning them with HR practices and policies.

REVIEW QUESTIONS

1 What is the relationship between employee engagement and retention?

2 Can you write your own definitions of employee engagement and positive organizational culture based on this chapter?

3 Can you list three intrinsic drivers of engagement?

Endnotes

1   Kahn, W A (1990) Psychological conditions of personal engagement and disengagement at work, *Academy of Management Journal*, 33(4), 692–724

2   Deci, E L and Ryan, R M (1985) *Intrinsic Motivation and Self-Determination in Human Behaviour*, Plenum Press, https://link.springer.com/book/10.1007/978-1-4899-2271-7 (archived at https://perma.cc/ZXY7-DM3N)

3   Kurt, S (2021) Herzberg's motivation-hygiene theory: Two-factor, *Education Library*, 31 March, https://educationlibrary.org/herzbergs-motivation-hygiene-theory-two-factor (archived at https://perma.cc/C5CV-YAJR)

4   Gallup (2025) What is employee engagement and how do you improve it?, https://www.gallup.com/workplace/285674/improve-employee-engagement-workplace.aspx#ite-357473 (archived at https://perma.cc/WY9Q-ZJ8C)

5   CIPD (2025) Organisational culture, www.cipd.org/uk/views-and-insights/cipd-viewpoint/organisational-culture (archived at https://perma.cc/FB7E-WFN8)

6   Prosci (2025) Kotter's change management theory explanation and applications, 2 September, www.prosci.com/blog/kotters-change-management-theory (archived at https://perma.cc/2PQH-FM7Z)

CHAPTER SEVEN

Employee relations

Introduction

Effective employee relations are at the heart of a healthy and productive workplace. Building strong relationships between employees and management fosters trust, reduces friction and enhances overall employee engagement, as discussed in Chapter 6.

In this chapter, we explore essential components of managing employee relations. First, we examine the foundations of employee relations management, including the collective and individual relationship between employers and their employees. We then move on to HR's role in managing employee relations, including issues such as advising on employment law, conflict resolution, absence management and supporting people managers. Communication skills are vital in employee relations, as they are the bedrock of activities such as negotiating, problem solving, relationship management and conflict resolution. We therefore consider communication skills and active listening in some depth alongside other vital skills such as emotional intelligence and creative thinking. We end the chapter by looking at the vital role of employee handbooks and HR policies in setting the groundwork for a transparent and compliant workplace. Well-structured policies help employees understand their rights, responsibilities and the organization's expectations. They also provide HR professionals with clear guidance on handling issues consistently and fairly, ensuring legal compliance and organizational alignment.

LEARNING OBJECTIVES

By the end of this chapter, you will be able to:

- Explain what employee relations involves.
- Describe HR's role in employee relations and how it differs from people managers' role.
- Understand the skills needed to be effective in the field.
- Evaluate your employee handbook and make suggestions for improvements.

Managing employee relations

> **Employee relations:** A term which describes the collective and individual relationship between employees and employers, with a focus on engagement, communication and workplace harmony.

Employee relations is an evolving field. It used to be understood solely in terms of industrial relations, focused on disputes between groups of employees and their employers and typically involving trade unions. Today, it involves managing the relationship between the employer and groups of employees as well as individual employees and includes such things as dispute resolution, performance management, absence management, as well as facilitating open, two-way communication between employers and the people who work for them. Employee relations can broadly be understood to fall into two categories: collective and individual employee relations.

Collective employee relations

Collective employee relations refers to the relationship between an employer and groups of its employees. Collective employee relations might involve pay disputes with large sections of the workforce, working conditions or, more positively, engaging groups of employees to feed into decision-making processes.

Collective employee relations can sometimes involve engaging with employee representatives, such as trade unions, which negotiate on behalf of employee groups. This is known as collective bargaining. The way that organizations manage this relationship can have far-reaching effects and have a significant impact on employee trust and organizational culture.

The extent to which employers engage employee groups in collective decision-making also has a huge impact on culture and employee engagement. For example, this could include employee representation on consultative committees (alongside managerial representation), such as one that provides guidance and recommendations to leadership on DEI matters.

Collective bargaining: When an employee representative, such as a trade union, negotiates with an employer on behalf of a group of employees on matters such as pay or working conditions.

Trade union: A group of workers from the same profession, industry or trade that come together to protect their rights and interests in the workplace. For example, one of the largest trade unions in the UK is UNISON, which represents people who work in public services.

Individual employee relations

Individual employee relations refers to the relationship between the employer and individuals within the organization. It might involve managing performance or certain behaviours, such as turning up late every day, frequently being absent or being rude and abusive towards other employees.

HR's role in employee relations

Employee relations is normally seen as falling within HR's remit. As a function, HR has an overarching view of the organization and can therefore ensure consistency in employee relations practice across functions and teams. Some organizations may have a specialist employee relations function (normally made up of HR professionals), or it may form part of the work of HR generalists. Even though overall responsibility for employee relations tends to lie with HR, day-to-day relations with employees fall to managers, so they have a huge impact on employee relations within an organization. A key role of HR is therefore to support managers with their team relationships and offer advice when necessary.

Managing employee relations is an art. It involves maintaining a positive and productive relationship between the organization and its employees. The benefits of effective employee relations are huge. It provides a harmonious work environment and feeds into high employee morale, high engagement levels and increased productivity. We will now look at some of the specifics of HR's role in managing employee relations.

Facilitating open communication

Open communication and facilitating employee voice are fundamental to effective employee relations. In Chapter 6, we considered how two-way communication between employers and employees is crucial for fostering an engaged workforce and building a positive, trust-fuelled and transparent culture. Organizations should encourage employees to voice their concerns, share ideas and provide feedback, and we considered many of the ways that could do this in Chapter 6, such as surveys, forums, focus groups and suggestion schemes.

Having a culture that encourages open dialogue is the starting point for effective employee relations. It shifts the perception of the employer and employee relationship from 'us and them' to a more collaborative one where the employer and employees work together to generate ideas, address issues and solve problems.

TOP TIP
Involve employees in policy formation

Look for opportunities to involve your employees in policy development, project planning and other critical decisions. It enhances employee engagement and satisfaction, as well as increasing buy-in to important policies and decisions from their inception.

Advising on employment law

A key part of employee relations work is keeping up to date with employment law so that you can advise managers when necessary on steps that they need to take. Employment law changes all the time, and keeping abreast of it is important. You first need to understand what has changed before figuring out how it applies to your organization and context, and then updating any policies and procedures as necessary. For example, a change to the law regarding employment rights and flexible working would need to be reflected in any flexible working policies and procedures. As an HR professional, you would also be responsible for highlighting the change to the organization and be prepared to advise managers when necessary.

STOP AND THINK

How do you and your colleagues keep abreast of changes in employment law? Do you feel confident that you would know about any changes in the law as they happen? How many of the following approaches do you take:

- Subscribing to HR-specific legal publications.
- Subscribing to CIPD updates on how to apply legislation changes.
- Regular training in legal matters.
- Signing up for alerts from professional associations or government websites.
- Seeking advice from specialists in employment law.
- Networking with peers and colleagues to share information.
- Reading recent employment law cases and thinking about how you would have approached a similar case had it been in your organization.

Formulating and advising on policies

HR formulates policies and procedures for the organization to follow. These need to comply with employment law and be easy to understand. Examples of HR policies are numerous and might include:

- Anti-discrimination policy.
- Flexible working policy.
- Remote work policy.
- Social media guidelines.
- Attendance and timekeeping policy.
- Internet and email usage policy.
- Performance evaluation and improvement policies.
- Disciplinary action policies.

Fair and transparent policies ensure employees feel valued and respected, and as such, this is a critical area of employee relations work. Consistency in applying policies builds credibility and trust within the organization, so this is a key role for HR.

Conflict resolution and disciplinary matters

Conflict resolution is a large part of employee relations work. It isn't typically taught in universities, and you are likely to develop the skill as you progress in your career. Many would say that conflict is an inevitable part of workplaces and there are many ways that it can show up. It can happen between the organization and individual employees, groups of employees or between employees themselves.

It's helpful to know about certain theories that relate to conflict resolution techniques. The first is human needs theory, which was developed by John Burton by building on Maslow's Hierarchy of Needs we discussed in Chapter 1. While Maslow identified physical human needs and saw them as a hierarchy, Burton and other needs theorists have argued that needs can be sought simultaneously – one does not need to be fulfilled before the next emerges. For Burton, conflicts are rooted in unmet human needs such as:

- Security – the need for structure and stability.
- Belonging – the need to be accepted by others.
- Identity – a person's sense of self and how others see them.
- Self-esteem – the need to be recognized by yourself and others as strong and competent.
- Personal fulfilment – the need to reach your potential.[1]

It's fairly easy to understand how unmet human needs, such as those listed above, could result in conflict at work. For example, understanding that conflict between two team members might be rooted in an unmet self-esteem or belonging need could be a great starting point for resolving disagreements. These needs are relevant in deep-rooted social conflicts that can arise in organizations, and resolution involves addressing these fundamental needs rather than surface-level issues. It is vital, of course, that you do not make assumptions. Being led by the facts and what you are being told, not by what you feel could be the root causes of problems.

Conflict can be formal (in the case of collective action with trade union involvement) or informal. It can also be managed formally, through set procedures, or informally. It can involve resolving conflict with an individual employee or with a group of employees (known as collective action).

Addressing conflicts early can prevent them from escalating into bigger issues. Managers should be trained to detect and recognize early signs of conflict and intervene promptly. By having open and honest conversations, managers should seek to identify the root cause of conflict, give accountability and work towards a resolution.

Creating a supportive environment encourages employees to address conflicts constructively. It's important for organizations to promote a culture of respect, inclusivity and collaboration to provide the right environment. Organizations can also provide resources such as employee assistance programmes (EAPs) and access to external counselling to help employees who may be struggling with conflict management.

Conflict resolution requires HR professionals to develop specific communication skills, which we consider later in the chapter. Managers' role in resolving conflict is key, and HR's role may also involve coaching and training managers to do it effectively.

MEDIATION

Mediation is a structured and voluntary process where a neutral person facilitates conversation between conflicting parties to resolve disputes. Mediators identify underlying issues, guide discussions and promote compromise. They do not try to establish facts or pass judgement on what should or should not have happened.

Mediation is a form of informal conflict resolution and is appropriate for situations such as personality clashes between team members or conflict that has arisen from a misunderstanding.

While mediation should often be considered as a first port of call, it isn't always appropriate. Consider a case where an employee has complained that their manager is making sexist jokes or demonstrating bullying behaviour. The power dynamics in this relationship are likely to make mediation an inappropriate course of action, and more formal disciplinary procedures may be necessary.

Transformative mediation is a theory developed by Robert A. Bush and Joseph Folger in 2004 and focuses on the empowerment of parties and the recognition of each other's perspectives. Transformative mediation is so-called because of its power to change how people behave after a dispute has been resolved. It contrasts with problem-solving mediation, which focuses on solving a short-term problem. Transformative mediation can result in deep changes in people and their interpersonal relationships.[2]

CONFLICT COACHING

Conflict coaching entails working with individuals to develop their conflict resolution skills. Coaches help employees understand their conflict styles, identify triggers and develop strategies for managing conflicts effectively. This approach empowers employees to handle conflicts independently and provides a longer-term solution.

A FRAMEWORK FOR MANAGING CONFLICT

Here is a proven conflict resolution framework you can use next time you are faced with helping to resolve a conflict.

1 Use active listening – we consider this skill in more detail later in the chapter. Actively listen to all parties involved without interrupting, show empathy and seek to fully understand their perspectives. This is particularly important when emotions are high and you, as an HR professional, need to create a safe environment for individuals to feel heard.

2 Consider mediation – either by yourself or a neutral third party.

3 Clarify roles and expectations – often, conflicts or misunderstandings arise due to unclear job roles, performance expectations or workloads.

4 Using a problem-solving approach – focus on finding a solution to the problem rather than assigning blame. This is a useful approach when you need to shift the focus from emotions to solutions and collaboration.

5 Encourage collaborative dialogue – conflict resolution is most likely to succeed when all parties commit to open and respectful communication and contribute to resolving the issue.

6 Consider a third party – sometimes conflicts are too complex or deep-rooted to resolve internally. In cases like these, when the conflict has been going on for a long time, an objective third-party perspective might be needed.

As an HR professional, you set the boundaries, rules and tone. You aim to restore the relationship between both parties.

TOP TIP
Look to the future

Conflict is rarely resolved with a single conversation or process. Once conflict resolution is complete, consider offering training and coaching to the parties involved to prevent further problems. This could involve training on communication or emotional intelligence to improve overall interpersonal dynamics.

HANDLING GRIEVANCES AND COMPLAINTS

> **Employee grievance:** A formal, written complaint from an employee that needs to be addressed by following a specific process and procedure.

> **Employee complaint:** A less formal complaint that may not need to be addressed formally within the organization.

Grievances and complaints are similar but not the same. A grievance can be thought of as an 'official' complaint. It needs to be addressed formally in the organization by following a set process, and usually involves an investigation to establish the facts and verify different parties' statements and beliefs. It then requires somebody to determine what should and shouldn't have happened and decide on appropriate action, given the findings and circumstances.

Ideally, most organizations hope to address any complaints informally, and normally without the involvement of HR, before they escalate. Many complaints can be dealt with this way, with the matter staying between the employee and their manager and the manager seeking advice from HR on how to handle it if necessary.

What's vital is that any employee concern is addressed promptly through timely resolution, to maintain trust and positive relations. Organizations should have a well-defined process for handling grievances and complaints, including providing multiple channels for reporting issues, conducting thorough investigations and taking appropriate actions.

Managing absence

A significant part of individual employee relations work is managing absence and supporting employees to attend work.

Some absences are planned, such as annual leave, and as such, are relatively easy for organizations to manage. Unplanned absences, however, create problems in terms of workload management and productivity.

An HR professional can be involved in absence management in several ways:

- Tracking employee absence metrics to understand absence levels and patterns (high levels of absence in an organization can indicate problems with culture, engagement or employee wellbeing).
- Implementing wellbeing initiatives to promote a healthier workforce and reduce absence levels, for example, mental health awareness programmes, gym membership schemes or fresh fruit in the office.
- Developing absence policies and advising managers on their content.
- Supporting managers in their role of managing absence, particularly with managing difficult conversations or complex situations such as health problems or personal issues.

The day-to-day aspects of absence management are normally the responsibility of managers in the organization, but they often require the support of HR.

TOP TIP
Get to know your organization's sickness absence

Understand your organization's sickness absence by taking the following steps:

- Read and review your sickness policy and process.
- Collate data on short and long-term sickness.
- Review whether managers tend to maintain contact with employees who are on long-term sick leave and keep records of their interactions. If not, that's an area for improvement.

- Look at short-term sick leave. Can you identify any common themes or reasons for employee absence?

- Given your findings, can you identify any interventions you could deliver which might reduce short or long-term absence?

- Review your absence data after three to six months and monitor any changes. What impact have your interventions had?

This is a great starting point to gain confidence in employee relations work before moving into more complex cases.

Managing disciplinary action

A key aspect of employee relations is managing disciplinary action when employees fail to behave in line with expectations set by the organization.

TOP TIP
Familiarize yourself with ACAS's Code of Practice

In the UK, the Advisory, Conciliation and Arbitration Service (ACAS) is a non-departmental public body which publishes a Code of Practice for managing disciplinary matters. All organizations must comply with and align their policies with the code. Search out the code and familiarize yourself with the key content.

Unacceptable behaviour from employees can range in severity, from consistently arriving late at work to bullying, stealing or acting in a way that damages the company's reputation.

HR professionals are responsible for formulating, updating and advising on policies and procedures related to poor behaviour and ensuring compliance with employment law. They work closely with managers who are usually responsible for setting behavioural expectations with their teams and managing disciplinary action when these expectations are not met. This line of work can involve some difficult conversations, and HR can add value by coaching managers on good practice, supporting them by attending meetings and advising them on employment law.

Managing employee performance

As we saw in Chapter 4, HR professionals are not directly responsible for managing employee performance, but they are responsible for advising managers on employee performance, highlighting key aspects of policies that managers need to be aware of and ensuring that performance management processes are fair, transparent and aligned with organizational goals.

Supporting people managers

As HR professionals, it's our job to ensure managers are trained to be able to do the right thing. This can be done via management training or coaching managers through the process (refer also to our discussion of people management training in Chapter 5). As an HR professional, you might be responsible for delivering the training, or it might be provided by an external trainer.

At first, delivering training can be daunting, but over time, your confidence will grow and you will become a subject matter expert and trusted advisor to the business. Remember the principles we discussed in Chapter 5 and keep training fluid and interactive to get the best out of everyone. Short, snappy workshops can work well. Longer, all-day training may occasionally be appropriate, but be mindful of fatigue and the potential for engagement levels to drop.

The advice and information you share with people managers must be up to date, and relevant (refer to the advice earlier in the chapter about keeping up-to-date with employment law).

The knowledge and experience that people managers have about laws and policies varies, so you must meet with them to understand where you can support them and what their training needs are. Your relationship with the people managers you work with is likely to evolve, and ultimately, you may be able to shift away from giving advice and more into coaching conversations, where you help the manager draw their own conclusions and find the answers themselves. Remember that this doesn't detract from your role or expertise, but demonstrates that the organization has competent managers.

Skills for employee relations

Employee relations work requires HR professionals to develop a huge array of skills. It involves negotiation, collaborative problem-solving, relationship management and conflict resolution. At the heart of all of these activities is the need to build trust and rapport with the people you are working with. And to do that, you need excellent communication skills, a high degree of emotional intelligence and creative thinking skills. We consider these below.

Communication

Being able to communicate well and help others to communicate well is a foundational skill in HR, and particularly in employee relations. Written and verbal communication skills are vital to do this role well. Policies need to be written in clear, concise language that avoids jargon and is easy to understand. Whether dealing with unacceptable behaviour, resolving conflicts, discussing absence with employees or advising managers on policies and employment law, being able to communicate well is foundational to your success.

Good communication is the starting point for building trust and rapport and collaboratively solving problems. Showing that you understand people's perspectives, empathizing, and communicating clearly without complex jargon will demonstrate that you care about the person you are working with and want to help resolve whatever issue is on the table. A key aspect of good communication is active listening.

ACTIVE LISTENING

Active listening is more than just hearing words. It involves consciously committing your entire attention to the person speaking, listening to the words they are saying, and watching for cues such as body language, facial expressions and their tone of voice so that you get the whole picture. It also involves responding to the speaker in a way that demonstrates you have understood what they have said, perhaps by paraphrasing them or asking a question to clarify or build on what you have heard. The idea behind active listening is that the speaker feels heard and understood. In a conflict resolution scenario, it can help to build trust, prevent misunderstandings and allow all perspectives to surface and be understood. Ultimately, it can lead to more effective problem-solving.

Emotional intelligence

Employee relations work often involves delving into thorny issues, resolving difficult problems or helping people through personal problems or unsettling issues such as poor health. It is emotional work, both for you and for those you are working with. It is vital to seek to recognize and understand others' emotions as well as manage and understand your own. This is known as emotional intelligence. Understanding others' emotions is part of active listening. It helps you to communicate better and build trust.

Creative thinking

Creative thinking can be a powerful tool when solving disputes and collaboratively solving problems to suit all parties. It enables more innovative solutions that might be more tailored to the exact problem at hand. This might make the solution more effective and sustainable.

The employee handbook and HR policies

> **Employee handbook:** A comprehensive document that outlines a company's policies, procedures and expectations.

In this chapter, we've talked a lot about the role of HR policies in employee relations. Organizations typically have a lot of policies and procedures that employees need to follow and as we've seen, HR professionals play a critical role in ensuring these are followed, and taking action if they are not.

The number of policies in organizations can be overwhelming, especially for new starters who have a lot of new information to remember. This is where employee handbooks come in. Employee handbooks gather all relevant policies and procedures together in one place. A valuable resource for employees, they ensure that expectations are clear and that all staff are managed in a consistent manner using the same rules. They also demonstrate that the organization is legally compliant. The days of handing a complete, physical handbook to new starters have long gone. Today, most organizations share this information in one place on their website. Not only does this enhance the employee experience, but as handbooks often begin with the company's history, mission, vision and values, it also contributes towards the employer's branding and culture, which we discussed in Chapter 3. Employee handbooks often include the following, although they vary between organizations:

- A welcome message from the organization's leadership – this sets the tone for the handbook and reinforces the company's commitment to its employees.
- Organization's history, mission, vision and values – this typically shows the organization's journey to date and explains the core values of the organization, along with some of the actions and decisions it has made.

- Code of conduct – sets expectations for employee behaviour, for example, dress code, professionalism, use of social media and ethical standards. Clear guidelines help maintain a respectful and ethical work environment and ensures everyone within the organization is aware of the protocols.
- EDI policies – all organizations are required by law to prevent discrimination, harassment and victimization. Putting these policies up-front demonstrates your commitment to these issues.
- Health and safety policies and procedures – these might include wellbeing and mental health resources as well as policies and procedures for staying safe while at work or when working remotely.
- Absence policies – outline the processes employees should follow when they need to be absent from work, whether a planned absence, like annual or parental leave, or unplanned like sick leave.
- Disciplinary and grievance policies and procedures – outline what happens in the event of a disciplinary procedure (including performance management) and how employees can raise a grievance.
- Pay and benefits – outlines pay periods as well as details about salary and bonuses and how pay is calculated.
- IT, email, social media and data protection policies.
- Whistleblowing policy – outlines how to raise concerns about malpractice confidentially and without facing consequences.
- Flexible and remote working policies.[3]

As an HR professional, your responsibilities surrounding the employee handbook include:

- Creating and updating the handbook and policies in line with employment law changes.
- Ensuring accessibility for all employees (e.g. printed copies, digital formats).
- Training managers on consistent policy application.

- Reviewing and communicating changes regularly.
- Maintaining legal compliance (especially with employment law in your jurisdiction, such as the UK's Employment Rights Act, Equality Act, etc.).

STOP AND THINK

Are you familiar with your organization's employee handbook? How helpful did you find it when you joined the organization? Review its content, bearing in mind what you have learnt in this section.

- Does it include all relevant information?

- How strongly does it reflect your employer branding and values?

- Can you see any areas where it could be improved?

CASE STUDY

An organization is facing multiple employee relations issues across sites, which are mostly to do with employees disagreeing with performance feedback and complaining about a lack of recognition. An internal audit found that employees felt ignored and out of the loop. HR subsequently received an increase in formal complaints and grievance submissions.

To address this, the HR team rolled out a four-part communication strategy aimed at improving employee relations. The team:

1 Reviewed internal communication channels and introduced a weekly bulletin for updates, policy changes and recognition shoutouts.

2 All managers completed training on active listening and feedback delivery.

3 HR launched a quarterly focus group hosted by regional HR reps as part of employee voice initiatives.

4 Leadership was made more visible with regional directors rotating monthly site visits for Q&A sessions.

WHAT WOULD YOU DO?
Number 7

You have recently joined an organization and have found that managers aren't following the company's policies and procedures. What's worse, the policies that do exist have not been updated for a few years. After highlighting the issue with your manager, you are asked to sort it out as soon as possible. How do you go about doing this?

CHAPTER SUMMARY

- Employee relations involves numerous activities and perspectives, including managing relations with groups of employees and individuals.

- HR's role is primarily to devise policies and procedures, ensure legal compliance and advise the business on putting policies and procedures into practice. HR professionals also play an important role in supporting people managers with employee relations issues within their teams.

- Communication skills are vital in employee relations and are foundational for succeeding in the role.

- The employee handbook is an important resource for clear and consistent communication of HR policies. It can also be a valuable tool for communicating an organization's values and culture.

REVIEW QUESTIONS

1 Write three ways that effective communication can support positive employee relations.

2 Name three benefits of managing employee relations through HR policies and conflict resolution

3 Name three things an employee handbook should seek to achieve.

Endnotes

1   Beyond Intractability (nd) Unmet human needs, Beyond Intractability, www.beyondintractability.org/bi24/needs (archived at https://perma.cc/5KPF-9GJ5)

2   Spangler, B (2013) Transformative mediation, Beyond Intractability, www.beyondintractability.org/essay/transformative_mediation (archived at https://perma.cc/DNK9-2HHL)

3   Solo, A (2025) Employee handbooks: Key policies and drafting tips for UK employers, Sprintlaw, 22 April, https://sprintlaw.co.uk/articles/employee-handbooks-key-policies-drafting-tips-for-uk-employers (archived at https://perma.cc/HLH7-WB3N)

CHAPTER EIGHT

Ethics, risk and governance and sustainability

Introduction

In this final chapter, we consider three vital components of HR practice that, as a strategic HR partner, you will need to think about every day – ethics, risk and governance and sustainability. HR plays a pivotal role in shaping the ethical framework, risk management and sustainability strategies in an organization.

The chapter begins by exploring ethics in HR practices and the principles that guide fair and responsible decision-making. From ensuring equitable treatment in recruitment to compensation to handling sensitive employee relations with transparency, ethics in HR is fundamental to building trust and credibility.

We then look at risk and governance in HR, highlighting how HR policies serve as a safeguard against legal, financial and reputational risks. Effective governance structures provide accountability, standardization and consistency in managing workplace environments.

Finally, we explore HR's role in corporate sustainability initiatives, embedding environmental, social and governance (ESG) principles into recruitment, employee engagement and workplace policies.

HR's role in these three vital areas is critical as we help shape and implement ethical practices, manage risk and governance and drive sustainability efforts.

LEARNING OBJECTIVES

By the end of this chapter, you will be able to:

- Explain what ethical practice means in relation to key areas of HR work.
- Describe the crucial importance of risk management and governance in HR, including areas of practice where it is needed and some risk mitigation strategies.
- Articulate HR's role in supporting and promoting sustainability initiatives, particularly concerning social and environmental responsibility.

Understanding ethics in HR practices

Ethical practice: The practice of applying ethical values to organizational behaviour, including all aspects of organizational conduct, such as employment practices, stakeholder relations, corporate governance and issues of product and corporate responsibility.

Ethical practice in HR involves conducting HR work with a moral compass, and ensuring that individuals are employed and managed fairly, respectfully, transparently and with integrity.

Ethics in HR is about ensuring that employees are treated with dignity, policies are applied consistently, and decisions are made with moral principles rather than solely being guided by legal compliance. It's also about protecting employee data and sensitive information.

Ethical HR practice supports a culture of equal opportunities and open communication, promotes a healthy and supportive work environment and holds leaders and employees responsible for ethical behaviour. As an HR professional, ethical HR practice requires you to develop your emotional intelligence skills to ensure you are making the right decisions for the organization. This can be both operational and strategic, as decisions you make today could have a longer-term consequence.

You should aim to be a role model and demonstrate ethical leadership and the behaviours of adhering to high moral standards in your work. This is important as it sets the tone and culture for the rest of the organization. HR should provide training and resources to support ethical decision-making and hold leaders accountable for maintaining ethical standards to promote a culture of integrity and trust. You can do this by having regular meetings with leaders across your organization to gauge how they operate in their business areas and constructively challenge anything that concerns you.

The CIPD has published a well-known Profession Map, which you are likely to be familiar with, that outlines expected knowledge, skills and behaviours needed by HR professionals. You might also remember that this map defines ethical practice as a 'core behaviour area', which the CIPD defines as 'building trust by role-modelling ethical behaviour, and applying principles and values consistently in decision-making'.[1] In 2015, the CIPD published research into ethical decision-making, listing eight 'lenses' to help practitioners in their pursuit to solve workplace problems ethically. The CIPD summarizes the lenses as:

1 Fairness – everyone in an organization should be treated fairly.
2 Merit – jobs and their rewards should track talent and hard work.
3 Markets – jobs and their rewards should follow from voluntary market exchanges.

4 Democracy – no one should be subject to a regime in which they have no say.

5 Wellbeing – work should be good for us.

6 Rights and duties – everyone has rights and duties not to violate others' rights.

7 Character – we should develop the best ethical character for our roles.

8 Handing down – we must pass on an undamaged world to our descendants.[2]

Ethical practice is highly likely to have been part of your studying, even if it may not have been obvious. But it will have been woven into your learning. Now that you are in the working world, you mustn't forget this moral aspect of your role. We'll now consider some key ways that HR professionals can embody ethical practice in some of the key areas of HR work we have considered throughout this book.

TOP TIP

Review the CIPD's Code of Conduct and Ethics

The CIPD's Code of Conduct and Ethics is available to download from their website. The CIPD encourages all its members to uphold the code, but it is also intended to guide anyone working in HR, whether they are a member or not.

Recruitment and selection

Recruitment and selection are the start of an individual's journey with the organization and related practices must be fair and non-discriminatory, by focusing on skills and qualifications rather than personal characteristics. We considered ways to reduce bias in the hiring process in Chapter 3. Transparent hiring processes, unbiased interview techniques and equal opportunity policies are essential for maintaining ethical standards. Even if you are not directly involved in recruitment, it's important to use your experience and knowledge as an HR professional to ensure the right practices are in place for your organization. The new recruit will move into their employee lifecycle and may at some point have an interaction or touch-point with you or your work.

Data collection

Organizations handle personal, confidential and sensitive information and data, and it must be collected, stored and used in line with data protection regulations. HR should implement polices to safeguard employee information and prevent unauthorized access. As an HR professional you must handle data correctly. This might just be as simple as ensuring you lock your computer or laptop, have passwords that are not easy to guess and a privacy screen protector on your laptop or monitor. Notebooks containing your personal notes should be kept in a safe place so that they don't end up in the wrong hands.

Compensation and benefits

We touched on the importance of fair and transparent compensation and benefits policies in Chapter 4. HR is reasonable for regularly reviewing and benchmarking compensation packages to ensure they are competitive and equitable.

Workplace harassment and discrimination

It's HR's role to educate, prevent and address workplace harassment and discrimination through clear policies and procedures. Regular training, creating a safe and respectful work environment and responding promptly and sensitively to complaints or concerns all helps to maintain ethical standards. As an HR professional, providing regular training to your managers and creating training modules for all employees is a good way to ensure ethical practices are followed.

Performance management

As touched on in Chapter 4, performance management and appraisals should be based on clear, measurable criteria and provide constructive feedback. Employees should have the opportunity to discuss their performance, set goals, receive support for their development and have a consistent framework. By working with integrity, you can ensure that ethical HR processes are being followed.

Employee wellbeing

Employee wellbeing and work-life balance are ethical responsibilities for HR. Organizations should offer suitable flexible working arrangements alongside wellbeing programmes and support for mental health. This needs to be advocated by HR, and as an HR professional, you should role model work-life balance behaviours to others across the organization.

STOP AND THINK

Reflect on your own team:

- How do you, as HR professionals, role model ethical behaviours to the rest of the organization? Can you think of any instances where you've seen evidence of this?
- Similarly, do senior HR leaders role model work-life balance or flexible working?

What risk and governance look like in HR

As an HR professional early in your career, you might feel that risk and governance aren't yet relevant to your role. The truth is, they are both highly relevant, and the earlier you start thinking about your involvement in and influence on these two vital areas, the better.

HR risk management

> **HR risk management:** When an organization identifies, assesses and puts in place mitigation measures for potential risks associated with workforce management.

HR risk management involves identifying, assessing and mitigating potential risks and threats to the organization. These could include:

- Compliance risks, such as failing to adhere to employment laws and regulations or undertake compliance training required by your organization's industry.
- Talent risks, such as failing to effectively manage recruitment, retention and succession planning, therefore leaving the organization at risk of productivity and, in some cases, continuous operational risks.
- Reputational risks, such as unethical practice, can harm your organization in the long term.
- Health and safety risks, such as failing to ensure workplace safety or employee wellbeing.
- Operational risks, such as failing to manage payroll effectively, or leaving yourself open to a cyber attack, so that you are unable to pay colleagues.

As with every department, the HR department has internal controls and conducts regular audits to manage HR risks. Establishing processes for monitoring compliance with policies, identifying potential risks and taking corrective actions all form part of HR risk management.

STOP AND THINK

Consider how your organization uses audits to manage risk. Seek out what audits exist, for example, payroll or benefits audits, and how regularly they happen. See if you can identify any gaps in auditing processes.

RISK MANAGEMENT AND MITIGATION STRATEGIES

Part of HR risk management is to develop and implement risk mitigation strategies. Examples could include:

- Succession planning to mitigate talent shortage risks.
- Safety training to mitigate health and safety risks.
- Data security measures to mitigate cyber attack or data breach risks, such as encryption, access controls, and regular data audits. HR should also provide training to employees on data protection to minimize the risk of data breaches.
- Crisis management and business continuity planning, to ensure that policies and procedures are in place to respond to emergencies such as natural disasters, pandemics, cybersecurity attacks, accidents and death. Practising and running through what would need to happen in these scenarios makes everyone aware of the emergency protocols and ensures that operations continue.

HR governance

HR governance: The policies, structures and frameworks that guide HR practices to ensure compliance, fairness and strategic alignment.

HR governance is concerned with the polices, structures and frameworks that guide HR practices. This can involve:

- Strategic workforce planning to align HR strategies with business goals.
- Talent management and development to ensure employees have the skills needed to succeed.
- HR metrics and analytics to measure HR effectiveness and inform decisions.
- Regulatory compliance by adhering to employment laws and ethical standards.
- Data security and privacy to safeguard employee data and ensure compliance with regulation requirements.

This last point is crucially important. Compliance with local laws and regulations is essential, for example, adhering to minimum wage laws, working hours and conditions, health and safety standards and anti-discrimination laws. As we've covered throughout this book, as an HR professional, it's important to stay informed about changes in legislation and update policies and practices to maintain compliance.

TOP TIP
Make sure you know your policies

When starting a new role, it's always good practice to read the organization's policies to help you better understand the tone and culture of the organization. It also allows you to review them and offer suggestions for improvements. This is a simple and easy way to start showing your value as an HR professional in the organization.

WHISTLEBLOWING

In Chapter 7, we covered how an organization's whistleblowing policy should be outlined in its employee handbook. Whistle-blowing protection is another key aspect of HR governance. Employees should feel safe to report unethical behaviour, violations of policies or illegal activities without fear of retaliation.

Having a clear whistleblowing policy and providing confidential reporting channels ensures concerns can be addressed appropriately.

> **Whistleblowing:** A term used to describe a scenario when an employee raises a concern about malpractice or unethical behaviour in the organization. It should be possible to do this confidentially and without fear of negative consequences.

> **TOP TIP**
> Get to know your organizations governance parameters and risk appetite
>
> Risk and governance in HR involves identifying, assessing and managing risks while ensuring compliance with legal and regulatory requirements. Each organization has its own thresholds and parameters for these, as well as risk appetite. This isn't always obvious and can vary drastically between organizations. If you're unsure where your organization stands, speak to stakeholders to understand it better.

> **STOP AND THINK**
>
> Do you have a risk and governance team in your organization? If not, who is responsible for risk and governance in your organization, specifically in relation to HR work?

HR's role in sustainability initiatives

If you feel a little confused about sustainability terminology concerning businesses, you are not alone. Over the years, terminology has shifted and evolved. The concept of Corporate Social Responsibility (CSR) has been around since the 1950s.

It emphasized ethical behaviour and organizations' social responsibility, but lacked any focus on the environment. Gradually, the concept of Environment, Social and Governance (ESG) began to take over, after the UN highlighted the importance of these three factors in investment decisions in a 2004 report called 'Who Cares Wins'.[3] ESG came to be broadly aligned with the term 'the triple bottom line', which refers to people, planet and profit. The idea is that businesses should measure their success according to the impact they have on society (people), the planet (planet) and their financial metrics (profit), rather than on financial metrics alone.

Today, ESG has evolved to the broader concept of sustainability, which refers to organizations' ability to sustain operations and succeed financially, while making a positive contribution to society, the planet and the economy. Organizations increasingly recognize the importance of integrating sustainability initiatives into their core strategies and measuring and reporting on sustainability performance is often a legal requirement, depending on your industry.

CIPD's 'People Profession 2030: a collective view of future trends' report predicts that sustainability will increasingly influence the future of work and the people profession.[4] In your current role, you might not feel that you have any involvement or impact on sustainability. After reading this section of the chapter, you will understand how everything you do centres around people, planet and profit. The role of HR in sustainability is to drive initiatives and embed responsible behaviours throughout the organization's culture. In addition, empowering employees with knowledge and skills related to sustainability enhances their personal ability to contribute to organizational initiatives.

People

Socially responsible HR practices include:

- Health (including mental health), wellbeing and belonging initiatives can address workplace stress and contribute to employee wellbeing and overall organizational sustainability.
- Community engagement, such as promoting employee involvement in volunteering programmes or fundraising.
- Ethical leadership
- Diversity, equity and inclusion initiative to create a supportive environment and enhance the social experience for everyone in the organization.

Socially responsible initiatives can have a hugely positive impact on an organization's reputation and employer branding, which we covered in Chapter 3. People increasingly want to work for organizations that value social causes.

Planet

HR can support organization-wide environmental initiatives by:

- Providing environmental awareness training to encourage colleagues to look at their own personal carbon footprint alongside that of the organization.
- Working with the organization to reduce the organization's carbon footprint and promote eco-friendly workplace policies, such as reducing water usage and responsible waste management.

Like socially responsible initiatives, environmental initiatives also feed into building a powerful employer brand to attract the right people to your organization.

Profit

As we have seen throughout this book, strategic HR involves aligning HR practices and strategies with business goals to ensure the long-term financial stability and viability of the organization.

STOP AND THINK

Reflect on your own team. Who is responsible for sustainability? Is there a separate team or an individual? Does it form part of your role? If not, can you identify any ways that you could start to support initiatives focused on people, planet and profit?

CASE STUDY

A global organization has strong growth and ambition plans but faces internal and external pressure about unclear ethical standards, inconsistent sustainability reporting and a lack of transparency in governance and decision making. The board and HR leadership implemented an integrated framework comprising:

- Ethics and values – it rolled out a global code of ethics and conducted mandatory training.
- Sustainability strategy – it established sustainability KPI's and launched Green HR initiatives.
- Risk management – it conducted a full supplier risk assessment and updated risk registers.
- Governance enhancements – it established a sustainability forum and publishes sustainability reports.

WHAT WOULD YOU DO?
Number 8

You have read a Glassdoor review of your organization that implied misconduct. What do you do?

CHAPTER SUMMARY

- By promoting ethical behaviour, managing risks, ensuring compliance and supporting sustainability initiatives, HR can contribute to the organization's long-term financial success and positive impact on society and the environment.

- Ethical practice in HR work is critical for setting the tone in the organization. We should aim to be role models and conduct all aspects of our work with a moral compass.

- Risks in HR work are significant but can be mitigated through thorough risk assessment and risk management strategies. It's important to understand your own organization's attitude to risk so that you can align your practice accordingly.

- Sustainability initiatives are concerned with people, planet and profit. HR can provide valuable support to the business in each of these three areas.

REVIEW QUESTIONS

1 Name three of the CIPD's eight lenses for ethical decision making.

2 Name three risks HR professionals need to manage.

3 What is whistleblowing?

4 What are the three main elements of sustainability in organizations?

Endnotes

1 CIPD (nd) Ethical practice, www.cipd.org/uk/the-people-profession/ the-profession-map/explore-the-profession-map/core-behaviours/ ethical-practice (archived at https://perma.cc/74M9-7NXC)

2   CIPD (2015) Ethical decision-making: Eight perspectives on
    workplace dilemmas, www.cipd.org/globalassets/media/comms/
    the-people-profession/profession-map-pdfs/ethical-decision-making-
    2015-eight-perspectives-on-workplace-dilemmas_tcm29-9564.pdf
    (archived at https://perma.cc/XBD2-BCSE)
3   ICL (2022) The evolution from CSR to ESG, 1 December, www.
    icl-group.com/blog/the-evolution-from-csr-to-esg/#:~:text=With%20
    so%20many%20companies%20eager,major%20career%20
    consideration%20for%20CEOs (archived at https://perma.cc/3W4V-
    JXJW).
4   CIPD (2020) People profession 2030: A collective view of future
    trends, www.cipd.org/uk/knowledge/reports/people-profession-2030-
    future-trends (archived at https://perma.cc/9KWR-2284)

Conclusion

This book has introduced the main components of HR for early career professionals working in the field. This concluding chapter aims to provide further guidance on your personal development journey, including how you can develop the skills, knowledge, competencies and behaviours that will support future activities in your HR work.

Developing your knowledge in the areas we've covered throughout this book is important. You may decide to remain as an HR generalist, or you may decide to specialize in one of the areas we have discussed, for example, talent acquisition. But having a grounding in all of these areas will help you to work collaboratively with colleagues and position yourself as a trusted advisor to the business. Bear in mind that new research frequently emerges, and HR professionals need to be able to adapt their approaches as work contexts change.

LEARNING OBJECTIVES

By the end of this chapter, you will be able to:

- Review and reflect on your skills in HR.
- Identify areas for future learning.
- Understand what the future might look like for HR professionals.
- Develop an action plan for continuous professional development.

Developing your HR skills

As an HR professional, you are responsible for your personal development journey and you will need to develop a wide variety of skills to help you thrive in your role. To develop the skills needed, it's important to equip yourself with the necessary technical knowledge, keep up to date with relevant research and legislation and source appropriate data within your organization. It's equally important to develop your 'soft skills' such as listening, speaking, verbal and written communication, organization, problem-solving, critical thinking and decision-making.

To further develop your career in HR, it is important to develop skills in conflict management, stakeholder management and handling sensitive conversations in a confidential manner, all of which we have covered in this book.

As an HR professional, it's vital you demonstrate integrity, discretion and take an ethical and inclusive approach to your work. It's also important to have business acumen and commercial understanding, as these skills help you look at the bigger picture and help you future-proof the work you deliver.

These mix of skills, behaviours and competencies will help HR professionals deliver value for the organizations they work for.

STOP AND THINK

Think about the topics we have covered in this book. Do any of them spark further interest? If so, consider exploring them further to become a subject matter expert. How could you do this in your current role? Identify specific steps and activities you could pursue.

Mental health for HR professionals

Due to the nature of the role, HR professionals are sometimes overlooked when it comes to participating in mental health initiatives in organizations. HR professionals often have to manage confidential information regarding colleagues, such as health problems, financial hardship or bereavement. They also manage difficult and sensitive situations such as bullying and harassment or redundancies. The role can be stressful and demanding at times, which can be draining, especially as an early careers professional navigating some situations for the first time. It's important that HR professionals put wellbeing and mental health strategies in place for themselves as well as others. It's important as an employee that you also engage and access support services such as employee assistance programmes.

TOP TIP
Look after yourself

Consider introducing self-care routines either daily, weekly or monthly to help you thrive in your role. This might be by taking regular breaks and getting outdoors, or spending time with family or friends to switch off from work. Putting things in place will help reduce the risk of stress and ultimately burnout.

KNOWLEDGE, SKILLS AND BEHAVIOUR ASSESSMENT – HR ESSENTIALS

The 'review questions' at the end of each chapter of this book will help you to assess your understanding of each topic discussed. A great way of assessing your HR skills is by rating yourself from 1–10 on knowledge, skills and behaviours for each topic, and completing it with your line manager. This will help you identify development areas and key strengths that you might not be aware of.

Ask yourself the following questions:

Knowledge

- Are you aware of current trends, research and good practices in each of the topics we've covered throughout this book?
- Can you summarize internal and external factors that affect or influence specific HR topics for the industry you work in?
- Do you understand any policies or procedures linked to specific HR topics?
- Do you know how to measure what good practice looks like or return on investment initiatives for specific HR topics?

Skills

- How confident are you in communicating the importance of specific HR topics to senior leaders and securing their buy-in for initiatives or recommendations?
- How effectively can you listen to employees' and managers' concerns relating to specific HR topics?
- Can you facilitate discussions about specific HR topics?
- Can you analyse data about specific topics and identify areas of concern or suggestions for improvements?

Behaviour

- How do you ensure you behave ethically in your HR work?
- How do you ensure that you are continuing your personal development as an HR professional?

TOP TIP

Below are ten top tips that can help you with your personal development to maximize your potential for future success.

1 Continue to develop your knowledge on specific HR topics, through professional membership, law updates etc. This will help you to continue to make good evidence-based decisions and advise your organization effectively.

2 Build your network, learn from other HR professionals within your team, attend events to build connections with industry experts.

3 Look at good practices and new ideas to keep up to date with HR topics.

4 Look for learning opportunities internally, and try to connect with more experienced colleagues to support your personal development journey.

5 Continuous learning is important, stay current on industry trends through online courses, podcasts, books and articles.

6 Engage outside of the HR department to learn about your organization and the industry it operates in.

7 Seek a mentor or coach internally or externally who can help you with your self-development journey.

8 Use data that is available and get familiar with it, build an in-depth understanding, so you can provide effective advice.

9 Take opportunities to build relationships with senior leaders within your organization; this will help you to position yourself as a trusted advisor to senior leaders and the executive team as you advance your HR career and increase your influence.

10 Take time to understand your organization's mission, values and objectives. Look at the work you do and create synergy through the work you do day to day.

The future of HR

HR is ever evolving, and it's important that you evolve alongside it. Ways of working can be influenced by changing economic, political, social or technological forces. While we can't accurately predict the future of work, we can make sure we keep up to date with changes. It is highly likely, for example, that technology and AI will continue to drive change in the years to come. Every HR professional, therefore, needs to take active time in horizon scanning, looking for possible changes that might affect their role, industry and organization. This will ensure that the HR function continues to add value and impact through the work they do. As key strategic advisors to the organization, this is vitally important. Here are some tips for early career HR professionals who want to future-proof themselves and their careers:

- Stay informed about emerging trends in technology and AI.
- Identify and follow trailblazing individuals who are looking at the future of work.
- Search for organizations that research and write about the future of work.
- Actively look for content on your own industry and how it will translate to future work you might do.

Wherever you can, start sharing your knowledge and insights with your team and managers in the organization. It will demonstrate your willingness and drive to keep the organization current and future-proof it. Don't forget, future-proofing any organization is everyone's business and responsibility, as it keeps everyone in their jobs.

Action planning for continuous professional development

As you have worked through this book, there have been opportunities for reflection, practical tips and exercises or recommendations for you to consider. The final step now is to reflect on what you have read, and think about your personal career development goals and ambitions in line with your current circumstances. You can do this by planning for your continuous personal development (CPD).

Your plan will be tailored to your circumstances, as it's individual to your experience to date and opportunities and goals.

Putting an action plan together can be daunting, as you are making a clear commitment to your personal development. It is worth it, though, and holding yourself accountable will help you to progress in your career.

Personal SWOT analysis

You may have heard of a SWOT analysis before. A personal SWOT analysis is a valuable tool for all HR professionals, particularly when they are in the early stages of their career. It provides a basis for personal reflection on strengths, weaknesses, opportunities and threats in relation to knowledge, skills and capabilities. Undertaking a self-assessment exercise can encourage you to stop, step back and reflect.

The SWOT analysis process is simple, and you can decide how in-depth you want your analysis to be. Begin by listing your strengths; what skills, knowledge and experience do you already have concerning the different aspects of HR discussed in this book. In the next section, we look at translating the personal SWOT analysis into a plan – this can include not just working on your development areas but further maximizing existing areas of strength. The second step is to reflect on your weaknesses, or development areas that you are aware of. Next, consider your opportunities. Are any particular career paths open to you in your organization, or are there any areas of HR work that you feel you are particularly suited for that you can pursue? Or is the best thing to remain as an HR generalist, given your own organization's context or set-up? Perhaps the best opportunity for you is to work your way up to be an HRBP.

Finally, look at potential external or internal threats that could prevent you from reaching your goals.

The most important part of your SWOT analysis is what you do next and how you determine the steps, actions or plans that you want to undertake as a result of it.

TABLE 9.1   An action plan for continuous learning

What is your specific objective?	How will achieving this objective support your HR career or ambitions?	By when will you achieve this goal?	How will you know when you have been successful?	What resources do you need to achieve your objective?

Action plan

Creating an action plan for continuous learning can help provide structure and clarity to your learning and personal development. It can help you identify goals, set timelines and break down what you want to learn into discrete, manageable steps. You can then easily track your progress.

Use your self-assessment reflections to help you, along with any of the other reflections you have undertaken as you have worked through this book. Use the template provided to set yourself some learning goals concerning your further development in HR. Aim to set yourself at least three objectives that can help to further your skills, knowledge or experience. Provide as much detail as possible when drafting your action plan and the specific goals within it.

Answers to 'What would you do?' exercises

This appendix gives suggested responses to the 'What would you do?' exercises included throughout this book. These exercises are designed to help you apply concepts in real-world scenarios and reflect on how you might approach practical challenges in a thoughtful, informed way.

Each answer offers an example of how a situation could be handled. They are not definitive solutions, but rather indicative responses meant to stimulate critical thinking and help you explore possible approaches.

You may find that your responses differ from the below, that's completely normal. Check out what's different and identify any gaps in knowledge.

What would you do? Number 1

You could prepare for the meeting by taking the following steps:

- Understand their background and approach by researching their previous experience through LinkedIn or previous companies they have worked for.
- Prepare to clarify your role and contributions, by outlining the projects or work that you have delivered, are currently working on and would like to get involved in the future. Show how you look beyond operational and reactive HR.

- Show openness to new perspectives and emphasize your willingness to support their goals and aspirations for the HR team.
- Position yourself as someone proactive and eager to grow under their leadership.
- Prepare questions you want to ask them to demonstrate your interest in the future of the organization and your role.

What would you do? Number 2

Structure your answers using the STAR method (Situation, Task, Action, Result) to clearly articulate your role, decisions made, and outcomes achieved. Reflect on specific cases you have handled: here are a few examples:

- Example 1: Navigating interpersonal conflicts between employees in the same team and facilitating mediation to restore working relationships.
- Example 2: Navigating change management where there are multiple demands and needs from the organization.
- Example 3: Long-term sickness case which has involved occupational health.

What would you do? Number 3

Start by asking the manager for examples of the underperformance. Ask if they have provided feedback to the new starter. If they haven't, ask why not, and if they have, ask if there been any improvement since the feedback was given. Improvement is a positive sign and suggests that performance is likely to improve with more support.

You could advise the manager to follow these principles when talking to the employee:

- Start with positives.
- Outline observations objectively.
- Provide specific examples.

- Set clear expectations moving forward.

Use the SMART model to construct the conversation that the manager needs to have with the new starter:

- Specific – Be specific about areas that need improvement and give examples of underperformance. Set clear goals for improvement.
- Measurable – Put measures against these goals that the manager and employee can use to understand expectations and measure performance.
- Achievable – The manager should ensure that both they and the employee feel these goals are achievable.
- Relevant – The goals must also be relevant to the person's role.
- Time-bound – Agree a timeframe for improvement with catch-up sessions to assess progress in between.

Finally, talk through the structure of the meeting and how they can approach the conversation, offering them the chance to role play with you to help build their confidence.

What would you do? Number 4

You could suggest that the manager approaches this conversation using the GROW coaching model. For example:

- **G** – Goal
  Example question: 'What specific improvement would you like to focus on in your performance?'
- **R** – Reality
  Example question: 'What challenges are you currently facing? What has worked well so far?'
- **O** – Options
  Example question: 'What approach could help you overcome this challenge? What support do you need?'

- **W** – Way forward
  Example question: 'What is one concrete step you will take this week? How can I help you stay accountable?'

What would you do? Number 5

Begin by asking the manager:

- Are you looking to identify future leaders, fill specific skill gaps or improve overall workforce effectiveness?
- What criteria currently guides your talent decisions?
- Are there any key business shifts in the short term and long term that are influencing workforce needs?
- Help the manager plot their current employees on the 9-box grid by discussing:
  - Leadership competencies and decision-making skills.
  - Ability to take on strategic responsibilities.
  - Innovation and adaptability in a changing environment.
  - Learning agility and willingness to develop new skills.

What would you do? Number 6

You could suggest the following to the area director:

- The use of pulse surveys or focus groups to understand employee sentiment.
- Regular check-ins between leaders and employees to foster transparency.
- Organizing team building activities that focus on collaboration rather than just socializing.
- Cross-functional projects to build stronger connections across teams.

What would you do? Number 7

A good process to follow would be:

- Assess the current state.
- Prioritize urgent compliance issues.
- Engage key stakeholders.
- Modernize policies and procedures.
- Roll out an awareness and training programme.
- Implement accountability measures.
- Monitor and adapt.

What would you do? Number 8

You could take the following steps:

- Investigate the claim, assess the validity, cross-check internal records and speak to stakeholders.
- Engage leadership and legal teams.
- Address employee concerns transparently.
- Manage public perception.
- Implement preventative measures.

Looking for another book?

Explore our award-winning
books from global business
experts in Human Resources,
Learning and Development

Scan the code to browse

www.koganpage.com/hr-learning-
development

Our Brand New
HR Skills Series

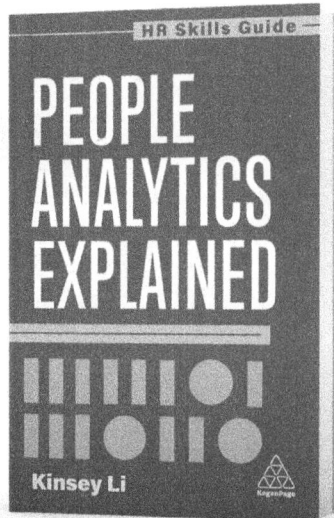

All the knowledge and
skills for your HR Career

KoganPage

From 4 December 2025 the EU Responsible Person (GPSR) is:
eucomply oÜ, Pärnu mnt. 139b – 14, 11317 Tallinn, Estonia
www.eucompliancepartner.com

www.ingramcontent.com/pod-product-compliance
Lightning Source LLC
Chambersburg PA
CBHW071606210326
41597CB00019B/3423

9 7 8 1 3 9 8 6 2 4 3 4 4